Singing

A Mennonite Voice

Singing

A Mennonite Voice

Marlene Kropf &
Kenneth Nafziger

Herald
Press

Scottdale, Pennsylvania
Waterloo, Ontario

Library of Congress Cataloging-in-Publication Data
Kropf, Marlene.
 Singing: a Mennonite voice / by Marlene Kropf and Kenneth Nafziger.
 p. cm.
 Includes bibliographical references (p.) and index.
 ISBN 0-8361-9152-8 (alk. paper)
  1. Church music—Mennonite Church. 2. Mennonites—Interviews.
 I. Nafziger, Kenneth James, 1941- II. Title.

ML3169.K76 2001
782.32'287—dc21   2001016781

Scripture is used by permission, with all rights reserved, and unless otherwise noted, is from the *New Revised Standard Version Bible*, copyright 1989 by the Division of Christian Education of the National Council of the Churches of Christ in the USA.

SINGING: A MENNONITE VOICE
Copyright © 2001 by Herald Press, Scottdale, Pa. 15683
 Published simultaneously in Canada by Herald Press,
 Waterloo, Ont. N2L 6H7. All rights reserved
Library of Congress Catalog Card Number: 2001016781
International Standard Book Number: 0-8361-9152-8
Printed in the United States of America
Cover and book design by Gwen M. Stamm

10 09 08 07 06 05 04 03 02 01 10 9 8 7 6 5 4 3 2 1

To order or request information, please call 1-800-759-4447 (individuals); 1-800-245-7894 (trade). Website: www.mph.org

To our children
and to our children's children
who sing.

Contents

Foreword

If an object were required to symbolize the Mennonite tradition, I would keenly suggest a pitch pipe. There are alternative possibilities that would accord with other strands of the tradition's witness—an open Bible, a towel, an olive branch. But I would opt for the pitch pipe, not for any inherent aesthetic potential, but because it enables the church to begin to sing.

And that, in brief, may well be the necessary vocation of Mennonites within the holy catholic church in the twenty-first century, especially where many Western Christians have substituted performance for participation, extolling the vocal or instrumental dexterity of a few and disdaining the voice of the congregation. This is especially true where churches have traded crafted texts and sturdy self-supporting tunes for pretentious jingles—the monosodium glutamate of hymnody—especially when one in four people and one in four churches in English-speaking countries of the Northern hemisphere don't believe that they can sing.

In 1993, I attended the annual meeting of the Hymn Society in the United States and Canada in Washington, D.C. It was there that I first encountered Mennonite music making as Ken Nafziger introduced items from *Hymnal: A Worship Book*. I remember even yet the physical sensation of being embraced by faith incarnate in song. It was the beginning of a continuing relationship with a tradition I have increasingly admired through engagements with Ken at Eastern Mennonite University and with Marlene Kropf at the Associated Mennonite Biblical Seminary.

I have been aware for almost a decade that this volume had been conceived and was in processes of gestation. Indeed, for the past five years I have referred to it as if it were already in print! So it is a pleasure to greet its birth.

What this book does is to provide that kind of necessarily anecdotal evidence that some scientific researchers may scorn, but that people of good sense recognize as essential. Percentages, graphs, and theories may be derived from accumulated information, but the life of faith is not easily put in a box or shown in a pie chart. The Holy Spirit is an unpredictable bird of love that nests in hearts, fertilizes imaginations, and reveals hidden truths according to God's will, not human prediction. What makes the same hymn inspire one individual to heroism and lead another to boredom cannot be calculated. It has to do with the mysterious way in which song connects us to our past, our soul, our future, our Savior. And because God intended us to be different, our uniqueness is caught up and reflected in our response to the music of the church.

So, here we can read at a leisurely pace the testimonies of God's everyday saints as they reflect on the relationship between their lives and the life of God as it is mediated, explored, and affirmed in song. And doubtless, as we read and reread these testimonies we will find memories recalled and insights confirmed where the pattern of another person's experience temporarily coincides with our own.

If this simply serves to reflect the varied experiences of people of faith, it will be sufficient. But God is always interested in the extra, and we should be too. I therefore dare to hope that this book will underscore the unparalleled importance of congregational song for the personal and public devotional life of their crafts to shape or misshape the faith of generations. I hope it will revitalize the belief that the most important music sounding in worship is the voice of the people.

Pray God that it will also confirm the Mennonite tradition as the pitch pipe that enables the rest of the church to sing.

—John L. Bell
The Iona Community
Glasgow
November 2000

Every hymn is a flare
of longing.

—*Cornelius Eady*[1]

Origins of the Singing Project

Let the word of God dwell in you richly; teach and admonish one another in all wisdom; and with gratitude in your hearts sing psalms, hymns, and spiritual songs to God.
—Colossians 3:16

Psalms and hymns were to be regarded as a method of teaching and admonishing; that is they were to be imbued with truth, and to be such as to elevate the mind, and withdraw it from error and sin. Dr. Johnson once said that if he were allowed to make the ballads of a nation, he cared not who made the laws. It is true, in a more important sense, that he who is permitted to make the hymns of a church need care little who preaches, or who makes the creeds.
—Albert Barnes[2]

Although the eight-year process of making a new hymnal for the Brethren, General Conference Mennonite, and Mennonite churches officially ended when *Hymnal: A Worship Book*[3] appeared in the summer of 1992, the ideas and questions that grew out of producing the hymnal eventually resulted, for us, in a two-year listening and research project in which we asked people in the church, "What happens when you sing?"

If there is wisdom to be found in this book, the fruit of that project, it is most certainly in the insights of the many gracious people who took time to speak with us about what happens as they sing in worship. Their responses told us at least two important things: first, that the assumptions we made in creating a new hymnal for our people were essentially correct; and second, that we should have asked all these questions *before* we started the hymnal rather than after it was finished. Perhaps the hymnal would not have ended up substantially different, but by asking these questions earlier, we might have saved ourselves the enormous effort we spent defining the criteria by which hymns would be judged.

The reasons that people sing would rarely please those for whom rational or theological or aesthetic arguments are necessary to support the inclusion or exclusion of a hymn. Neither would the answers please those for whom literary excellence is a prime concern; the sensibilities of liturgists, seminarians, and musicians whose thresholds of tolerance are narrow would likely be offended as well. Had we conducted these interviews before compiling the hymnal, rather than the other way around, our list of criteria would likely have been shorter, more subjective, and based more frequently on the experience of singing a hymn together rather than on the analysis of its parts by some objective means. For in our interviews, we heard that matters of experience, association, and the challenges of hymn singing are often most important to people who sing. We heard that the physical pleasure of singing is prized, that images that speak to a person's life are useful handles, and that singing is the most important activity in which people engage in worship.

More than one hundred people in the United States and Canada were interviewed in this research project, and the conversations were taped and transcribed for study purposes. A few interviews were done in writing.[4] The total number does not include the many additional people—Mennonites and non-Mennonites—who volunteered stories and thoughts as they heard, through private conversation or in public gatherings, about this project. Interviews were usually an hour and a half long, sometimes more—and sometimes much more. We found additional stories in church publications that appeared around the time of our research.

We sought to include a wide representation from throughout the Mennonite churches: the people ranged in age from ten to eighty-something; most were not professional musicians (though a few were); some were born and raised Mennonite and others chose as adults to become Mennonite; and their congregations represented a variety of worship styles. We make no claim, however, that this is a scientific study. There may indeed be Mennonites who think differently about singing than do the ones quoted in this book. We should say, though, that there was remarkable, fundamental agreement on the most important questions we asked—namely, the ones having to do with the importance of singing in Mennonite worship and experience.

Interviews were conducted as informal conversations. Most covered the same topics, but we allowed the nature of the conversation to dictate its direction. Thus, identical questions were not used in all interviews. However, the basic questions used were these:

- What does music do to and for the individual and the congregation?
- What happens between you and God as you sing?
- What happens between you and others as you sing?
- Are there specific hymns that are or were important to you? Why?
- What is the earliest hymn you remember? Why?
- What hymn is a recent addition to your list of favorites?
- Have you reclaimed hymns that you had earlier discarded?
- Are you transported when you sing? Where have you gone?
- What makes a hymn work or keeps it from working?
- What do you give to a hymn? How are you taken by a hymn?
- What active responses have hymns inspired?
- Who is the God you sing to?
- Are there hymns that are hard or impossible for you to sing?
- When do you need to sing?
- Are there holy places when you sing? Holy times? Holy visions?

Most of the interviews were completed in 1994 and 1995. Material from these interviews has been used in workshops over the past number of years—a practice that tended to produce more conversations and more stories. Marlene incorporated some of this research into her doctor of ministry project, *Singing as Sacrament: An Exploration of the Role of Hymn Singing in Mennonite Spiritual Formation.*[5] Together, we organized material based on these interviews for "Why Mennonites Sing," the keynote address at the annual conference of the Hymn Society in the United States and Canada, held in July 1997 in Savannah, Georgia.

We are deeply indebted . . .

. . . to all the people who so graciously made their time, their experience, their memories, and their words open to us in the interviews;

. . . to all those who, having heard others' stories, contributed stories of their own;

. . . to all the parents, grandparents, uncles, aunts, and other singers in the church who passed on an important tradition to us;

. . . to the places we work—Associated Mennonite Biblical Seminary and Mennonite Board of Congregational Ministries (Marlene) and Eastern Mennonite University (Ken)—for their encouragement of this project;

. . . to Jeremy Nafziger, editor (and Ken's son), whose skill with words and understanding of music and love for both rearranged our unwieldy and dissonant manuscript into a harmonious whole of four parts;

. . . to institutions such as the Glen Eyrie Conference Center (Colorado Springs, Colorado) and Laurelville Mennonite Church Center (Mount Pleasant, Pennsylvania) that provided space for writing;

. . . and to the One who gives us breath and pulse that so easily and so willingly get changed into song, just as miraculously as water got changed into wine—and the finest wine at that!

I get the feeling I'm sinking
into a feather bed when I
come back into the sound
of Mennonite singing.

—*Ann Graber Hershberger*[1]

Part One

The Sound and Sense of Mennonite Singing

I owe the Lord a morning song 651

GRATITUDE CM

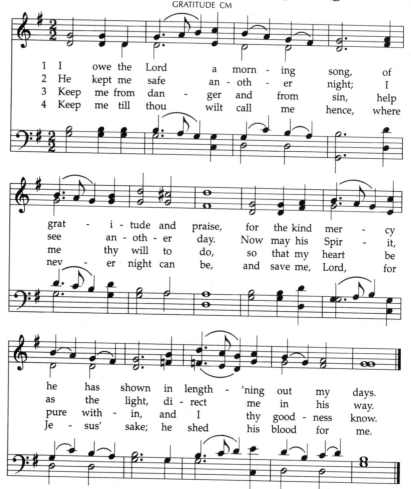

1 I owe the Lord a morn - ing song, of
2 He kept me safe an - oth - er night; I
3 Keep me from dan - ger and from sin, help
4 Keep me till thou wilt call me hence, where

grat - i - tude and praise, for the kind mer - cy
see an - oth - er day. Now may his Spir - it,
me thy will to do, so that my heart be
nev - er night can be, and save me, Lord, for

he has shown in length - 'ning out my days.
as the light, di - rect me in his way.
pure with - in, and I thy good - ness know.
Je - sus' sake; he shed his blood for me.

Text: Amos Herr, *Hymns and Tunes,* 1890
Music: Amos Herr, *Hymns and Tunes,* 1890

What Is This Sound?

The space is simple, unadorned. People sit quietly on wooden benches. Here and there children squirm or swing their feet. Then the sound begins, warm as summer rain, substantial as mountains. The congregation is singing, and sound fills the space, reverberates, rises. For a moment, earth touches heaven.

What is this sound? What is this song?

Like the sturdiest Shaker furniture, "I owe the Lord a morning song" (No. 651) reflects the simplicity of an earlier Mennonite era's approach to the composition of music for the congregation. Its beauty resides in its being functional; its longevity is due to the solidness that allows, even invites, a congregation to return to it again and again.

Mary Oyer, executive secretary of the Joint Hymnal Committee that in 1969 assembled *The Mennonite Hymnal*,[2] told the story of the hymn like this:

> Amos Herr (1816–97), a Lancaster County preacher and advocate of the use of English in worship, wrote the text. Unable to get to church on one snowy Sunday morning, he praised God with a new text. *Hymns and Tunes* [*for Public and Private Worship*, published in 1890] indicates that "Gratitude" was written by the committee; at any rate no one claimed the sole responsibility. The *Church and Sunday School Hymnal* of 1902 credited *Hymns and Tunes* with the music. The editors of the *Church Hymnal*, 1927, inserted Amos Herr's name for both text and tune, an attribution continued in *The Mennonite Hymnal*, 1969.
>
> This might be called a typical (Old) Mennonite hymn. Its language is simple, straightforward, and functional, presenting abstractions rather than concrete images. Like most pre-electricity morning songs, the text expresses relief that the night has passed and uses day and light as symbols for enlightenment and heaven.
>
> "Gratitude," set in Aiken's seven shapes or character notes for easy reading, would have been a fine, simple song for singing schools. The bass part is limited to four notes. The sopranos cover

21

one octave, but the inner voices use only five and six notes. Yet the simplicity does not mean dullness; the tune wears well.

In its simple way, "Gratitude" makes a kind of journey and a return home again. It does so with its question and answer phrases and its key signature. The first phrase is answered rather inconclusively by the second, which moves to a new key. The third phrase begins again with a slightly different question which is answered decisively this time. The key changes are standard for a short hymn, but they contribute to the "journey." The first half of the music adds one sharp to the sharp of the signature. The second half cancels the sharp of the signature with the natural. Thus in a brief time we make a balanced excursion around the keynote (G), and we come to the end with a sense of having departed and come home again.[3]

When congregations sing this hymn, they produce a "typical Mennonite sound." What is that sound? One cannot reproduce it on one's own, except in memories.

Going Home to Oregon

Marlene:

Recently I went home again. On Sunday morning I worshiped in the Mennonite church of my childhood—a large, plain, wooden building without steeple or ornament that sits on a hillside in the small town of Sheridan, Oregon. I hadn't been back on a Sunday morning for at least thirty years.

In this church, everyone waits quietly for the service to begin. There is never a prelude because there are no musical instruments. In those moments of waiting, I look around the meetinghouse and remember my baptism, my wedding day, many funerals, and the ordinary Sunday worship services of my childhood.

On this morning, my younger brother, the newly ordained pastor of the congregation, is the worship leader. He opens the service with words of welcome and a prayer. My nephew, a lad of twenty, is the song leader of the day. He stands to lead the congregation, now shrunken from the three hundred I remember to seventy or eighty hardy souls. I have a moment of anxiousness as I take the hymnbook from the rack. It is the old navy blue *Church Hymnal*, the same hymnal I sang from as an adolescent. What will the sound be like?

My nephew announces the hymn in a clear, confident voice. He lifts his arm to direct, and the music begins—the first hymn in the hymnal:

Come, thou Almighty King,
help us thy name to sing . . .

I sing only one phrase, and then I'm choked with tears. So I listen. Yes, the sound is still there: sturdy bass voices providing a firm foundation, clear tenors, plain sopranos—not light or delicate but confident, unafraid of high notes. The altos? They seem a bit weak, so I begin to sing again.

Then I watch my nephew. His song leading is a little awkward, but he has the pulse, and the people follow. He learned music as I did, just as everyone has always done in that congregation: by listening, observing, and being there since he was a babe. When I look more carefully, I recognize in his posture and movements the song leaders who preceded him—his father, as well as Abner, Archie, Doris, and all the others—the song leaders I grew up with. It was always men who led singing in the worship service, but women were allowed to lead in Sunday school. No matter who was leading, we all sang with full voice, full heart.

The sound is still there. And I am grateful.

Going Home to Ohio

Ken:

I grew up in Central Mennonite Church of Archbold, Ohio. Every Sunday I saw around me my immediate neighbors: the farmers with whom my father threshed and made hay, the women with whom my mother quilted and canned, and many who were blood relatives. Having done other things together as a community for the intervening six days, our coming together under the same roof for several hours on the "day of rest" was an important extension of that community.

The Sunday school hour began with adults and children singing together. When classes were dismissed to go to the basement, another period of singing followed, this one just for the children. Then when everyone reconvened in the sanctuary for worship, there was more singing. Songs were chosen by the song leader, and anyone could predict the day's hymns and how well or poorly they'd be sung as soon as the song leader emerged with the preachers from the prayer room behind the pulpit. The hymns were chosen mostly from the gospel song tradition and occurred each Sunday morning at the same places and in the same quantities.

The seating arrangement in my church was one that encouraged learning to sing parts. The women sat on one side; the older women in the amen corner and toward the front of the outer aisle; middle-aged women and women with children in the center and back of the outer aisle; young women nearer the center of the middle aisle; and the girls toward the front of the middle aisle. The men and boys sat across the aisle in an arrangement that mirrored the women. So as young people found their way into the singing traditions of the congregation, girls were always surrounded by sopranos and altos; boys, by tenors and basses.

In parts was the way you heard singing. The notion of reading music never crossed my mind, so that when I auditioned for junior high school choir and the teacher said that he wanted me to read music for him, I panicked. He handed me a sheet of music and said, "I'd like you to sing the tenor part." My panic was immediately relieved, because I knew I could sing a tenor part. What I didn't know was that reading music meant singing a tenor part or that it was considered a sophisticated skill.

Many other opportunities to sing together occurred outside of the Sunday morning meeting. Sunday night services included singing. Some of these services were hymn sings, appreciated by all ages. The older people especially enjoyed singing from the *Church and Sunday School Hymnal*; the younger people preferred the newest gospel songs from the Singspiration publishers. And there were yet more chances to sing: Wednesday night prayer meetings, Mennonite Youth Fellowship meetings, quartets, trios, choruses. The musical life of the congregation was actively supported, and in my recollections, widely enjoyed.

The details of our musical life were not appreciably different from those of other Mennonite congregations across the country. We shared a common understanding of music, a common practice of music, and a common repertoire of hymns.

What Would You Do Without Music?

One of the questions we asked the people we interviewed was: What would you do if someone decided that from here on out there would be no more singing in worship?

Their answers were quick and from the gut. Here is a sampling:

"Do you mean, what would I do besides leave?"

"I'd find another church."

"It would rob us of our church. We couldn't go to a church that didn't sing. Singing is the glue that holds worship together."

"I think it wouldn't even be church. I would think I was in the wrong place. I'd probably react violently. We'd all be dead and gone. No one could stop us."

"I get so weary of words. The reason I go to church is to sing."

"I'd sing in my head."

"If I wasn't allowed to sing, I'd rebel."

"Without music, I wouldn't want to go to worship anymore. I would feel as if I were dying. My prayer book would have been taken from me."

"Worship without music sounds joyless, comfortless, cold."

"I would be robbed of a certain intimacy with God."

"I'd dry up. It would feel like something is being squeezed out of me. Even as you ask the question, it's like someone putting a vice on me and draining everything out of me. I'm even getting short of breath now. I wouldn't last long."

The reasons for these answers were in all likelihood related to these answers to a question about the role of music in worship:

"Sometimes sermons don't connect with what is going on in my life. In music there is always a home, a place where I can lose and find myself or find meaning."

"Music is the hinge between heaven and earth."

"Singing a hymn might be the holiest moment of the whole service."

One person confessed that she is a Mennonite *because* of the singing. She said:

I went to another church for a while that wasn't Mennonite. I really liked their theology better, but frankly, I just couldn't stay there because there was no music. It was pathetic. I even tried leading singing there, but the sound didn't come back to me, and I didn't know how to get it. It seemed hopeless, so I came back to the Mennonite Church.

Another person said:

Every year I attend the Easter Eve vigil in a nearby Roman Catholic basilica. The service is stunning—dramatic scripture readings and processions, an incisive homily, a marvelous brass ensemble—but every year I come away with an empty spot in my heart. I always think, "If only I could have this splendid liturgy with Mennonite singing, then I would be in heaven."

George R. Brunk II, probably the most famous Mennonite evangelist, affirmed the critical role of singing in his revival campaigns.

I believe the singing drew many people to the meetings—the animation [and] spirit [of it]. I don't think people were [excited] from the preaching—that was the singing. I don't know that I'm qualified to explain any psychological relationship, but it's a studied fact that just making music lifts the spirits of people and enables them to engage in true worship, and this prepares the way for exposition of the scriptures.[4]

Some of the interviewees were asked:

If you had to choose between singing and preaching in worship,
which would be the last to go?

They all had the same answer, although many hesitated before responding. Typically they said something like, "Well, I know I
should say that preaching would be the last to go. The truth is,
music is more important to me than preaching."

"Music can speak where sermons just cannot," one woman said.
"It touches people more often." Even seminary professors and
preachers gave that type of answer. "How do I get in touch with
spiritual things in worship?" said a prominent Mennonite theologian who has preached scores of sermons. "Because I'm so cerebral,
I'd think it would be hearing a sermon or preaching a sermon myself. But the most powerful thing is music."

For many Mennonites interviewed, there is little in corporate
worship that *needs* to be done that cannot be done by singing together. Singing can gather the congregation; it can become the vehicle of praise, confession, and intercession; it can speak the word
of God; it can transform and empower a people. It not only carries
the actions of worship forward, it *is* the primary action of worship.

What became abundantly apparent is that in the absence of a
weekly eucharistic tradition, singing functions for Mennonites as
sacraments do in liturgical churches. Singing is the moment when
we encounter God most directly. We taste God, we touch God
when we sing. It is an occasion of profound spiritual experience,
and we would be bereft without it.

Songs We'd Take with Us
Learning the music of the people is learning their faith.
—Linda J. Clark[5]

We asked each interviewee for this project: What, if you were
banished to a remote island, would be the hymns you would take
with you? What are the hymns that hold special memories for you?
Their answers were swift, sure, and often passionate. And, as for

Isaiah and his temple experience that he dated by saying "In the year that King Uzziah died . . .,"[6] momentary experiences of singing specific songs can stand like milestones or trail markers along the path of a person's life. One person described the process of singing memorable hymns as "bringing the past to the present and enjoying it." She said she could take anything from the hymnal, so long as the selections represented something from each part of her life.

To sing again any of those treasured hymns enables the singer to return to both the time and place where those associations happened and to bring to the present moment those other experiences as well. Often when singing one of those hymns, nothing else matters: the eyes fill, the pulse races, and the singer's immediate surroundings are replaced by the experience of the past. One respondent suggested that how we learn songs is a bit like falling in love; that is, you can fall out of love with a person or a song and leave that person or song, but the *where* and *when* of falling in love is a one-time thing and not forgotten.

At the conclusion of his play *Dancing at Lughnasa*, Brian Friel puts these words in one actor's mouth:

[T]here is one memory of that Lughnasa time that visits me most often; and what fascinates me about that memory is that it owes nothing to fact. In that memory atmosphere is more real than incident and everything is simultaneously actual and illusory. In that memory, too, the air is nostalgic with the music of the Thirties. It drifts in from somewhere far away—a mirage of sound—a dream music that is both heard and imagined; that seems to be both itself and its echo; a sound so alluring and so mesmeric that the afternoon is bewitched, maybe haunted by it. And what is so strange about that memory is that everybody seems to be floating on those sweet sounds, moving rhythmically, languorously, in complete isolation; responding more to the mood of the music than to its beat. When I remember it, I think of it as dancing. Dancing with eyes half closed because to open them would break the spell. Dancing as if language had surrendered to movement—as if this ritual, this wordless ceremony, was now the way to speak, to whisper private and sacred things, to be in touch with some otherness. Dancing as if the very heart of life and all its hopes might be found in those assuaging notes and those hushed rhythms and in those silent and hypnotic movements. Dancing as if language no longer existed because words were no longer necessary.[7]

So too is it many times with the memory of singing not just a hymn, but a certain hymn, in a certain place, with certain people—even on a deserted island.

"Great is thy faithfulness"

"Great is thy faithfulness" (No. 327), in Mennonite experience, seems able to do all this more than any other hymn. No song was more often mentioned in these lists of important hymns. One person summarized in a few words what many people said about this hymn: "The text is just wonderful, and the musical setting has everything that a hymn should have." At Forest Hills Mennonite Church in Lancaster, Pennsylvania, the combined adult Sunday school classes were invited to call out their favorite images from the text. In no time at all, nearly every word and every image rang out. The text contains very little that can be called extraneous, and the truths of its poetry are confirmed by what singers know from biblical sources; thus, little time need be wasted to wrestle with theological or poetic ambiguities.

The music for "Great is thy faithfulness" is strong enough to bear the repeated singings and the weight of many levels of memory. The tune is memorable, the harmonies rich (like God's faithfulness of which the text speaks), and all the parts (even the alto!) are interesting and rewarding to sing. Many congregations and even more individuals can sing all three stanzas by heart. The hymn is "a wonderful expression of one's relationship to God and vice versa," one person said. "I get quite emotional when I sing this one."

At the mention of "Great is thy faithfulness," Henry Buckwalter recalled an occasion when he was in Belize on a church service assignment:

> I don't know if I was going through a difficult time, [but I remember] going out and sitting on the wall by the sea and singing that song.... That was twenty-eight years ago, and the picture comes back just like that. A couple weeks ago, we sang that at my sister's funeral, a sister who died prematurely at age fifty-one of cancer. There have been different experiences along the way like that. That to me is one of the most beautiful hymns that's ever been written.[8]

327   Great is thy faithfulness

FAITHFULNESS 11 10. 11 10 with refrain

1 Great is thy faith-ful-ness, O God my Fa-ther. There is no
2 Sum-mer and win-ter, and spring-time and har-vest, sun, moon, and
3 Par-don for sin and a peace that en-dur-eth, thine own dear

shad-ow of turn-ing with thee. Thou chang-est not, thy com-
stars in their cours-es a-bove, join with all na-ture in
pres-ence to cheer and to guide, strength for to-day and bright

pas-sions, they fail not. As thou hast been thou for-ev-er wilt be.
man-i-fold wit-ness to thy great faith-ful-ness, mer-cy, and love.
hope for to-mor-row; bless-ings all mine, with ten thou-sand be-side!

Refrain

Great is thy faith-ful-ness! Great is thy faith-ful-ness! Morn-ing by

Text: Thomas O. Chisholm, *Songs of Salvation and Service*, 1923
Music: William M. Runyan, *Songs of Salvation and Service*, 1923

morn-ing new mer-cies I see. All I have need-ed thy

hand hath pro-vid-ed. Great is thy faith-ful-ness! Lord, un-to me!

"I owe the Lord a morning song"

Another hymn called for in this imaginary trip, though not as often, was "I owe the Lord a morning song" (No. 651), introduced earlier in this chapter. It is a beloved hymn, especially among older people. Some had experiences of singing it somewhere only to be surprised that no one other than Mennonites knew it, and that, having once heard the hymn sung, the others wanted to hear it again or to learn it. Daniel Suter said that singing this hymn while on a bus trip in Nova Scotia "struck a real chord with people. They had us sing that song every morning from then on."[9] He recalled that the hymn was sung often in his family and in his church for as long as he's been going to church.

During a cross-cultural semester of study in Germany, a group of Eastern Mennonite University students attended worship at the Weierhof Mennonite Church. The congregation, as part of their welcome, asked the students to sing for them. After the group abashedly acknowledged that there was nothing they could sing together from memory, the congregation asked for "I owe the Lord a morning song." Again, when it was clear that the students didn't know this from memory either, the congregation sang it—all four stanzas, and in English! They had learned it from PAX boys[10] who worked in that area after the Second World War.

For God so loved us 167

GOTT IST DIE LIEBE 10 9 with refrain

1 For God so loved us, he sent the Sav - ior. For God so
2 He sent the Sav - ior, the bless'd Re - deem - er. He sent the
3 He bade me wel - come; oh word of mer - cy! He bade me
4 Glo - ry and hon - or, O Love e - ter - nal, to thee be

loved us, and loves me too.
Sav - ior to set me free.
wel - come; oh voice di - vine!
giv - en while life shall last.

Refrain

Love so un - end - ing,

I'll sing thy prais - es. God loves his chil - dren, loves e - ven me.

1 Gott ist die Liebe, lässt mich erlösen.
Gott ist die Liebe, er liebt auch mich.

2 Ich lag in Banden der schnöden Sünde,
ich lag in Banden und konnt nicht los.

3 Er sandte Jesum, den treuen Heiland,
er sandte Jesum und macht mich los.

4 Jesus, mein Heiland, gab sich zum Opfer,
Jesus, mein Heiland, büsst meine Schuld.

Refrain   Drum sag ich noch einmal:
Gott ist die Liebe,
Gott ist die Liebe,
er liebt auch mich.

Text: August Rische, *Gott ist die Liebe*; tr. Esther C. Bergen (Sts. 1-3), *The Youth Hymnary*, 1956, copyright © 1956
Faith & Life Press. Used by permission. *The Hymn Book* (St. 4 and refrain), 1960
Translation (St. 4 and refrain), ©1960 *The Hymn Book*, Kindred Press, 4-169 Riverton Ave., Winnipeg,
Manitoba R2L2ES. Used by permission.
Music: Thuringer melody, ca. 1840

"Gott ist die Liebe"

Hymns and songs people learned as children left vivid memories. "For God so loved us" (No. 167), just as well known by its German title, "Gott ist die Liebe," was mentioned a number of times. Lee Snyder, president of Bluffton (Ohio) College, described the context that was common for a number of people who had learned this song as young children. "German was spoken by the older people in the congregation," she said. "My grandparents would have spoken German, but I didn't know German. But we learned that song, and it became a link into something that was no longer part of that congregation but was still a valued part of the tradition."[11]

A host of memories and impressions surround this hymn for folk singer Chuck Neufeld:

> The Austrians sang this in a different way. Instead of "Drum sag ich noch *ein*mal . . ." ["Therefore I will say one more time . . ."], they sang "Drum sag ich *tausend*mal. . . ["Therefore I will say a thousand times . . ."] . . . ."
>
> Now when I sing that song, I'm in Linz, Austria. The memory is me in the church service sitting on wooden benches without backs on them in the midst of looms that had been set up to teach refugee women the skill of weaving and behind me was a woman who was breast feeding a baby. That image, the ultimate image of nurture, is always there. Partly because of my curiosity as a little boy from a tradition where breast feeding would not have been done so openly, but that's the image: sitting there with the other boys and girls, singing that song with great exuberance.[12]

For Chuck, maternal images of God were rooted in the experience of singing this hymn.

"Praise God from whom"

Any Mennonite worth his or her salt is bound at some point to ask, "And what about 606?" "Praise God from whom" (No. 118) did appear in the comments of many people, falling into three general categories best described as "I must take it with me," "I'm somewhat embarrassed to take it with me," and "I'd be glad to leave it behind."

118 Praise God from whom

DEDICATION ANTHEM (606)

*Alternate phrases: Praise God from whom all blessings flow, praise God all creatures here below, praise God above, ye heav'nly host

Text: Thomas Ken, *Manual of Prayers for the Use of Scholars of Winchester College*, 1695, altered 1709
Music: Boston Handel and Haydn Society Collection..., 1830

*Alternate phrase: O praise our God, bless'd Three-in-One

606, so named for its location in the 1969 *Mennonite Hymnal*, quickly came to be the best-loved of all Mennonite anthems across the country. It is a setting of the Thomas Ken doxology to the music of a nineteenth-century American anthem found in Lowell Mason's *Boston Handel and Haydn Society Collection* (ninth edition, 1830). Its style is imitative and significantly more complex than most hymns; it is high and brilliant and energetic in rhythm. In large and small churches alike, it called forth the best in Mennonite congregational singing—the sound was more vigorous, more engaged. John Ruth, Mennonite pastor and historian, once referred to the sound of this hymn being sung as "the sound of Mennonite community."

As an icon of cultural identity, 606 was threatened as word spread that a new hymnal was in the works. "Will 606 still be 606?" was asked often of committee members. Sometimes the question was facetious, but most times it seemed to be the voiced part of a question that was really, "Will this new book take away or in any way threaten our tradition of singing?"

The hymn, whose inclusion in the new book was never a question, was assigned to the "Praising/Adoring" portion of *Hymnal: A Worship Book*. "Praising/Adoring" was made the second section of the hymnal and thus "Praise God from whom" received the odd-sounding low number of 118. The Millersburg (Ohio) Mennonite Church, one of the first churches where the new number was revealed, good naturedly but roundly booed and hissed the announcement. But regardless of the hymn's location, the people still sing "606"—not "118."

Those who wouldn't leave home without their 606 cited many and varied reasons: it is sheer pleasure and a rewarding challenge to sing; it has been used as an important ceremonial piece that has made many gatherings memorable; it is simply unthinkable to leave it behind. Someone suggested that it would make no difference to be alone with 606 because the memory of how the parts sound together could still make the experience complete.

Those who were somewhat embarrassed to consider 606 as one of the few things they might take to their remote islands called attention yet again to the pride (excessive) that Mennonites seem to take in having mastered this thing. These people might believe we've made of it too much of a show piece, that it's the only thing we can think of when we're asked to sing something on the spot or when we're in a place where we'd really like to try out the acoustics. Some have held it up as the epitome of Mennonites' need to sing all the notes right. These criticisms surface from time to time, sometimes because 606's flamboyance runs in direct contrast to the images of modesty and restraint that Mennonites also claim. There are those who argue that such complicated music is bound to keep newcomers away. Michael Bay, a Mennonite musician of Pentecostal background, observed that singing this type of hymn can be

> . . . an exercise where everyone worries about singing the parts and the rhythms correctly. But [with 606], they know the parts so well that they aren't tied to the music any more. There is freedom when you know it so well that you get beyond the performance of music and let what's inside of you come out.[13]

Those who would be happy to leave 606 behind, a small but vocal minority, generally cited their own weariness at the thought of singing yet another 606. But if their sisters and brothers are to be trusted—and if they should be allowed to return from their exile on a remote island—606 will likely still be around, ready to provide for them an exuberant return.

And Many Others

Many other hymns found their way onto people's lists of songs they would take with them. Stories in which a hymn coincided with an important or emotional event sometimes made that hymn unleavable. For example, Esther Augsburger spoke of her father's love for "My Jesus, I love thee" (No. 522):

> It was his favorite, and now I find it a little more difficult to get through it without tears. About three days before he died, a group of young people from James Madison University were going to have a reunion after ten years of meeting together. These were students he had discipled and with whom he had held Bible studies in his home. Sometimes there were fifty kids sitting around on the floor. Sometimes he went with them to rock concerts dressed in his plain coat and black hat.

On the day they were to have their reunion, he was in the hospital on his death bed, but his mind was clear. He said he was disappointed that he didn't get to be at that reunion. I asked him, "Would you like to go?" And he said "Yes." So we had an ambulance take him there. The kids had their guitars and they were singing. He was on his stretcher, and he was so weak that he couldn't talk that loud. Each one of the students filed by him, and he talked with each one. At the very end, he asked if they would sing, "My Jesus, I love thee." So they sang the first two verses, but they didn't know the rest by heart, so they stopped. He, with a strong voice, sang through the last verse:

> [In mansions of glory and endless delight
> I'll ever adore thee in heaven so bright.
> I'll sing with the glittering crown on my brow.
> If ever I loved thee, my Jesus, 'tis now.][14]

The experiential comments that people made about hymns and hymn singing offer insights as to how a singer and a hymn "fall in love." That experience is often sudden and unexpected and usually lies completely outside the control of the person who is smitten. Ken remembers, as a child, sobbing for the baby Jesus, who in "Away in a manger" (No. 194) has to sleep with the animals in a barn. Here is a sample of how some interviewees described this sense of intense connection with a song:

"'There's a wideness in God's mercy' (No. 145) speaks to me right now and reminds me that perhaps God's way of looking at issues is slightly different from ours. It frees me."

"When we sing 'Sing praise to God who reigns' (No. 59), the voice of the congregation together affirms who God is."

"Once while singing 'O little town of Bethlehem' (No. 191), I was struck by the line 'be born in us today,' as if I had never noticed it before. It explained to me what Advent, coming, and incarnation are all about. I listened for the rest of the song."

"In 'O God, great womb of wondrous love' (No. 155), finding a God who mothers has been very nurturing and healing."

"I enjoy singing 'O Power of love' (No. 593) for its strong melodic character, for its powerful text, and for the richness of the bass part."

"In 'Who is so great a God' (No. 62), I'm singing to an infinitely big, wonderful being. Many times I'm singing to the adjective."

"In 'Praise to God, immortal praise' (No. 91), I am moved by the contrast between the blessings and the difficulties which are expressed in these verses. This is the only song I can play on the piano."

"Singing 'Lift your glad voices' (No. 275) at my father's funeral made me feel the support of the congregation. I also felt the affirmation for someone who had given so much to the church and that he had joyfully entered the next life."

"I have a daily litany of hymns for myself: 'I come to the garden alone' for the morning; 'The church's one foundation' (No. 311) for noontime; and for the evening, 'How great thou art' (No. 535, *Mennonite Hymnal*)."

"There's a complexity to 'Be thou my vision' (No. 545); it has body; it has dimension."

"When my husband and I and another couple traveled in Ireland, we found these wonderful small chapels in out-of-the-way places. At one place, we needed to enter the chapel by getting down on our hands and knees to crawl through the small entrance. Once inside we sang 'Be thou my vision' (No. 545) as our very private and moving worship service. When we sang it [again recently], I was immediately back in that small chapel in Ireland."

"'A wonderful Savior is Jesus' (No. 598) gets me to think deep, getting where you find stuff that might sometimes be uncomfortable, but in the larger sense of being hidden."

"The words of 'When peace like a river' (No. 336) are us communicating to God, but maybe in some way the music itself is an avenue that God uses to communicate back to us something within our spirits."

"There's something about the beauty of the music of 'Praise, I will praise you, Lord' (No. 76). It's simple in its articulation of theology, and yet it's sound—praise, love, serve."

In "Jesus, priceless treasure" (No. 595), several people found the thickness of Johann Sebastian Bach's harmonies and the independence of the four parts to be an important way of expressing the individual within the totality of the community, and important as rich food for the soul.

Many have already found favorites among the international hymns in *Hymnal: A Worship Book*. Through the Mennonite World Conference that meets every six years, Mennonites have been introduced to the music of many of the world's cultures. Music is always an important representation of the variety in this whole body of the church. Also, many Mennonites have spent time in service work around the globe, and the music from these other cultures returns them to those places. Some who learned the hymn in Spanish as "Tú has venido a la orilla" insist that singing "Lord, you have come to the lakeshore" (No. 229) in English doesn't do the hymn justice. Some, especially from the General Conference Mennonite tradition, find it equally unrewarding to sing the German hymns "Wehrlos und verlassen" ("In the rifted Rock I'm resting," No. 526) or "Ich bete an der Macht der Liebe" ("O Power of love," No. 593) in English.

The richness of story and personal expression in response to the interview questions shows the multifaceted and powerful event that goes on when a congregation sings together. People can be in many places simultaneously, they can be in many different years at the same time—all while appearing to be singing with the rest of the congregation in a very typical Sunday morning worship service. Only our hearts know where we are when we sing together. And perhaps at times, even the heart is surprised. "Singing has me often meeting God at very unexpected times," Ron Guengerich said.

> All at once the music and the words hit me, and I can't sing. I'm glad there are people around me who can continue singing the words while I get a grip on myself. Why am I so affected? It would take me twenty minutes to go through what I heard in those few words and that wonderful sound.[15]

No one seems in the least bothered by this experience during the singing of hymns; most regard it as an enrichment of the act. To pay attention in hymn singing therefore means an attentiveness to all those levels of meaning *and* an involved awareness of all that goes on immediately around the singer *and* singing pitches, rhythms, and words *and* listening to the music *and* surrendering one's self to the experience *and*. . . . Small wonder that we would need to or want to sing a hymn more than once, or that from time to time we would find a hymn that we'd like to take with us on the journey.

Holy Sounds and Holy Places

Marlene:

In the past, I have often taken our singing tradition for granted. Wrapped in the sound of a cappella singing from my earliest memories, I—like many Mennonites—never questioned its power nor seriously explored the reasons why we sing. All that changed as I served on the council that compiled *Hymnal: A Worship Book*. I began watching people sing. I listened to what they said about particular hymns and then about singing in general. Eventually I became curious enough to join in this research project.

Why do Mennonites sing? Probably for the same reason all people sing: we enjoy it. Singing is a human activity first of all, not a churchly activity. Sometimes in the making of our hymnal, after all the arguments for or against a hymn had been made, someone would simply say, "But our people *like* to sing that song." And that would be enough to get the hymn voted in.

But there is something deeper, of course. Even though Mennonite worship has been plain to the point of barrenness and utterly devoid of the typical trappings of sacramental liturgy, a favorite hymn of several generations (sadly missed when it was excluded from *The Mennonite Hymnal* and brought back by popular request in *Hymnal: A Worship Book*) has been "In thy holy place we bow" (No. 2), written by two Mennonites near the turn of the twentieth century:

> *In thy holy place we bow,*
> *perfumes sweet to heaven rise,*
> *while our golden censers glow*
> *with the fire of sacrifice.*
> *Saints low bending, prayers ascending,*
> *holy lips and hands implore,*
> *faith believing and receiving*
> *grace from thee whom we adore.*

Holy light doth fill this place;
Spirit, light our way to guide.
In the presence of thy face
sin and darkness ne'er can hide.
Heaven's gleaming, fullness streaming,
life and truth for all are found;
light pervading, never fading,
lighting all the world around.

On thy holy bread we feed,
hunger never more to know.
Thou suppliest all our need;
Savior, whither shall we go?
Ne'er forsaking, here partaking
bread our souls to satisfy;
here abiding and confiding,
we shall never want nor die.

When I watched what happens when people sing this hymn, I wondered: How could this hymn attract such a devoted following among a people who banished incense and were congenitally suspicious of holy light, holy bread, and holy places? One could look at technical aspects of the hymn—evocative symbolic language, biblical resonances, pleasing internal rhymes, a satisfying tune, interesting and accessible harmonies—and catch some glimpses of its appeal. But none of these nor the combination of them all fully accounts for the reverence and awe that descend upon a congregation that sings this hymn from memory, the faraway looks in people's faces, or the silence that fills the room when the last chord dies away. What is obvious is that the Holy One has come near, and anyone who is even half awake notices it.

Because of that hymn and others like it, I was compelled not only to go home again but to ask my people across North America: What happens when you sing?

Human speech is like a
cracked kettle on which
we tap crude rhythms
for bears to dance to, while
we long to make music that
will melt the stars.

—*Gustave Flaubert*[1]

used w/choir
8/2001

Part Two

What Happens When We Sing?

307 Will you let me be your servant

THE SERVANT SONG 87. 87

1,6 Will you let me be your ser - vant, let me
2 We are pil - grims on a jour - ney, we are
3 I will hold the Christ - light for you in the
4 I will weep when you are weep - ing, when you
5 When we sing to God in heav - en, we shall

1,6 be as Christ to you? Pray that I may have the
2 trav - 'lers on the road. We are here to help each
3 night - time of your fear. I will hold my hand out
4 laugh I'll laugh with you. I will share your joy and
5 find such har - mon - y, born of all we've known to -

1,6 grace to let you be my ser - vant too.
2 oth - er walk the mile and bear the load.
3 to you, speak the peace you long to hear.
4 sor - row till we've seen this jour - ney through.
5 geth - er of Christ's love and a - gon - y.

*Guitar chords for unison singing only

Text: Richard Gillard, 1976, alt.
Music: Richard Gillard, 1976; adapted by Betty Pulkingham
        Text and music copyright ©1977 *Scripture In Song* (a div. of Integrity Music, Inc.) /ASCAP. All rights
        reserved. International copyright secured. Used by permission. c/o Integrity Music, Inc., 1000 Cody
        Road, Mobile, AL 36695.

Singing Creates the Body of Christ

The effect of voices joining together to sing is noticed when the singing is especially good, but otherwise often taken for granted. When some African communities build a new communal space, they routinely check the acoustics before giving final approval to the work. If the room sings well, it is acceptable because, potentially, every voice of the community can be heard.

Breathing Together

When Mennonites were asked what happens when they sing, they didn't talk about God first. Instead, they talked about what happens on the horizontal level—the human connections that occur. That connection happens first on a physical level—interactions of the voice, ears, mind, and heart. Cynthia Lapp described the energy created by a group singing together:

> It was a hot, sticky evening. Fans were trying to move the air in the Associated Mennonite Biblical Seminary chapel where a group of Sacred Harp singers had come to sing for a hymnology class taught by Mary Oyer. We all struggled along trying to read this "new" kind of solfege, figure out the rhythms, listen, and at the same time block out this strange way of singing. By the end of the evening my clothes were sticking to me, my throat burned from singing in such a raw way, and I was exhilarated.[2]

Poet Jean Janzen, who wrote several new texts for *Hymnal: A Worship Book*, said:

> Our Mennonite music is the taut rope that pulls us through every possible situation. . . . It's not only a rope given by God, it's a rope we make strong with our faith, our voices, the contributions we throw into things—our words, our efforts, our music. There's a George Herbert poem that says

> > *But Thy silk twist let down from heav'n to me,*
> > *Did both conduct and teach me, how by it*
> > *To climbe to Thee.*[3]

That's a pretty accurate description. With a hymn we are actually given something to hold on to, a kind of survival piece.

Jean went on to describe this "survival piece" as the connections that happen on a physical level.

8/2001

When we sing, we all use our bodies. We all lift our lungs; we breathe in and out together; we keep the pitch together. What I am doing with my body connects me with other bodies—even bodies of the past. We sustain the spirits of the past through this physical act of singing.[4]

A young woman recalled that among her earliest memories is her father holding her against his chest and saying, "Feel the vibrations as I sing." She remembered the comfort that came from that singing. That same manner of comfort was offered by her grandparents, her parents, and now by her brothers and sisters to their own children. Another interviewee, a woman in her eighties, said that she has always responded very much to the rhythm of the music. "I still do that," she said. "This old woman ought to just stand there quietly, but I have to respond to the rhythm of the music."

"It's a question of acoustics," said another person, a ham radio operator by avocation. "When you hear something coming back at you, you hear your own voice blended with another's and the regenerative effect that it has. The more feedback you have, the more you feel like feeding it and making it happen."

Many people we spoke with found ways of talking about the larger-than-life feeling one gets when singing. A woman described singing as "being overwhelmed with the immensity of life, and that seems like the presence of God. It's not just this body and this blood and these bones, but something is moving through me, connecting me to everything else around me." Another person observed that "if you are honest in singing, it always seems to call forth more. Singing has been the ultimate way of worship, because it's a body working together rather than one person doing it for me, or me doing it for them."

Some spoke of the immediacy of singing, an awareness of the

sounds as they first fall on the ear of the singer/listener. Lee Snyder said she finds

strands of sensual experience [running] through a cappella singing, though we never talk about it. Basses and tenors singing with sopranos and altos—that's a very sensuous thing. Sometimes that is what I'm thinking about when I'm singing. When I listen to wonderful voices around me, I am always curious who is singing. I try not to be rude and turn around and look. It's very mesmerizing, it's very attractive, and a lot like sexual attraction between men and women.[5]

When the interviewer asked, "Those voices are the equivalent of fingerprints, right?" Lee said, "Right, but fingerprints aren't very sensuous!"

People singing together release powerful energies, compelling and very difficult to resist. A hymn at the conclusion of conference gatherings or church-wide festival events; "Lift your glad voices" (No. 275) as the final hymn of a funeral; the elaborate version of "All hail the pow'r of Jesus' name" (No. 285) at any time; the first hymn at the beginning of an academic year; communion hymns (in particular "When I survey the wondrous cross" [No. 259 or 260] or "I am the Bread of life" [No. 472]); those moments of extreme tragedy or joy in a congregation's life: These are the times when the members really need each other to sing together. "Any statement of faith that is expressed by one and heightened then by thirty or by two hundred or by five thousand people becomes absolutely phenomenal," said musician Marilyn Houser Hamm, a member of the Hymnal Project's Music Committee. "And when people find themselves entering so fully into an expression, the expression moves beyond them, and they move through music into the realm of the spirit."[6]

Merle Good, a native of Lancaster County, spoke of the intertwining of the physical and spiritual dimensions of sound when he told the story of his father's ordination:

I remember when my father was ordained by lot, which is a very good memory, that we sang, "Have thine own way, Lord" (No. 504). The church was packed, lots of people were crying, and you had this sense of all the different political factions in the congregation. One of the great things about the lot is that everyone gets to nominate their person, and there is a process of examination, and then it's, "Lord, it's your call." There is something of a folk quality about that, but it also has an extremely spiritual quality about it that we lack in this academic age. Whenever I hear that hymn, it certainly brings back that sense of committedness. My dad didn't want to be a preacher, but then he was—all of a sudden.[7]

New York City pastor Ruth Yoder Wenger explored a similar theme:

When we sing together, there's some sort of energy that grows out of who we are, out of the music, out of the words, out of being together, out of God's presence, but it's greater than any of those. It's what draws us back into who God is and who we are in God. I have this sort of ethereal notion that God sets a melody for us, and we join in the harmony and the rhythm and the rhyme with our music. And since God calls us all to harmony and has created us in harmony, when we sing we resonate with what God has already set in the universe. We sing with the stars of the morning, and we sing with the saints of heaven.[8]

Crossing Boundaries of Time

Song can be understood as a special form of wisdom. Like wisdom, song seems to have been present with the Creator from the beginning of time. It is a constant delight to the Creator and rejoices in the presence of God. Those who love song, like those who love wisdom, inherit wealth. And like wisdom, song is remembered: when powerful sounds have been sung, the resonance does not end. Many with whom we spoke could return to certain moments of song by force of memory or by singing the same hymn in another time and another place. The body is involved with the singing of the moment, but the spirit leaps across the bounds of time and distance and recovers still-resonating sounds. Some could recall, by singing a hymn with such associations, the light or temperature or humidity of the occasion they remembered.

A cappella

by Shari Miller Wagner

As we gasp between lines
a chasm opens
from the older hymns.

I sense a darkness
like what I heard
at an Amish barn door,

the entrance to a church
or a cavern
where my ancestors

droned the poetry
that could not be uttered
in the village.

In sixteenth-century
dungeons
they sang these hymns

as a way to connect
flesh chained to walls
and racks. We hold

these broken ones
in our voices
like bread that could

bless us. Grandma Mishler,
whom we buried
the Easter when hyacinths

bloomed inside ice, leans
behind my left shoulder
and Shawn with the quick

laugh who died
giving birth
sits beside Grandfather

on the couch. They listen
with their eyes closed.
All of the old ones

are here in the dark
room of a house that
stood where corn grew

because God sent
the sun. We end with
"Praise God from Whom

All Blessings Flow"—
the version with echoing
alleluias and amens.

We don't need the book
and no one sets the pitch.
We've sung this one

at every marriage
and funeral. Even in-laws
with eyes on the last

five minutes of a game
join in from their corner.
From every direction

there are voices within
voices, husks beneath
husks. The dead sing

in a house so haunted
we breathe
the same breath.[9]

The physical act of singing together creates a bond not only in the present but with memories of the past. One person said:

> I like this *with* feeling very much—the sense of history I feel in a lot of hymns. The cloud of witnesses feels very strong—mother and father, uncles and aunts that I left early in my childhood. I know the stories and the heritage, having worked on a family history. I feel the voices now of my cousins in Russia. I love it when we sing really old texts because the old voices are present.[10]

For many interviewees, certain songs were able to take them far away, to people they loved or once knew. One said:

> I think as you get older, memories begin to matter more. Even songs that you may not like still become a link to a place or person or event. If I sit down in the evening with the old *Life Songs* hymn book, I sing one song after another. And I'm back at my home church sitting where I sat as a child. I'm not outside the church looking in; I'm inside and it's full of people.[11]

Lois Kauffman, in a magazine article, described the power of a hymn to take her to a long-ago place and time:

> One Sunday evening when I was just a little girl, I was standing by my mother in Plum Creek Mennonite Church. We were singing "Savior, breathe an evening blessing" (No. 209, *Church Hymnal*). It had been a hot, dry summer, but that day we had rain and it cooled off. Cool breezes of that freshly washed air with just a hint of wild rose petals blew in through the open window. Now, seventy years later, every time I hear that song, I am a little girl again, standing by my mother and smelling that wonderfully fresh air.[12]

Hearing Amish people sing prompted one man to write about early memories of singing in his childhood church:

> Who could sing like Uncle Orval? I never heard another person who could,
>   until last year.
> Sometimes us kids tried to run our sounds together in imitation,
>   but it never sounded right.

Maybe other men couldn't because they were too young
and were without memory,
or they didn't have the ability.

Who wanted to sing like Uncle Orval?
God knows, I liked his sound.
It was rich, as strong and solid as his body,
as textured and substantial as his bushy eyebrows.
It seemed to start deep inside him, circle around inside
his head
and finally roll out of his mouth and nose:
each pitch and word touching the one before
and the one after it,
connecting the song from beginning to end.

You had to follow Uncle Orval's lead because it was always there,
strong, distinct, and out front when the congregation sang—
all alone, like a night beacon,
when everyone else paused to breathe.
I used to wonder whether he was able to sing the whole song with
one breath.

Recently I heard Amish singing.
As the foresinger slurred through the notes and words of the hymn,
I was transported back to Harrisburg, a child again,
listening with fascination through adult ears
to Uncle Orval leading the congregation.
Since then, I've wondered if he alone was keeping a fading
tradition,
singing for all his worth a memory of his youth,
the last voice of our forgotten past.[13]

Learning to Sing

Many who were interviewed had little difficulty retrieving their
first memories of singing—both at home with their families and at
church. They remembered singing quartets around the piano at
home, or memorizing hymns during family devotions at the dinner
table, or lining up outside a brick meetinghouse at summer Bible
school to march in singing "We're marching to Zion."[14] And they
remembered the people who passed on this wondrous gift.
One woman remembered "sitting on the couch with my mom

every evening and singing through every song in that little red children's songbook."[15] A man said that one of his most cherished possessions is a cassette recording of his mother's lullabies that she made for the family before she died. He also remembered looking on while his older brothers and sisters gathered to play musical instruments. Because he was too small to play a real instrument, they made him a kazoo—a comb with waxed paper on it—so he could play along. Another person used to play church with siblings: "We would sit with our dolls on the staircase, pretend we were in church, and sing every song we could remember."

In some people's memories, singing was linked to work. "My 'singing faith' developed as a farm lad when I sang all the songs I knew to the cows and in the fields," said a seminary professor. One woman remembered that her mother used songs to send messages: "She sang to give us comfort, to put us to sleep, and also to inspire us to work. I remember her singing the line, 'There is work for us all and excuses for none!'"

Another person recalled:

I can hardly remember a time when I was not singing. Both of my parents loved music and music making, so singing

Marlene:

The bed my sister and I shared was covered with a multicolored patchwork quilt made by one of our grandmothers. Since she and I were sometimes sent to bed before we felt like going to sleep, we delayed the inevitable by playing a game.

One of us would find a square of fabric on her side of the quilt and ask the other, "Can you find a patch like this one?" When the matching fabric square had been found, the finder could choose another design and repeat the challenge. Later when we grew tired of the quilt game, we would snuggle under the quilt and sing through our entire repertoire of songs—mostly hymns but also American folk songs our mother had taught us. Eventually Dad would knock on the door, interrupt our singing, and remind us it was time to go to sleep.

Perhaps it was these bedtime songs that prompted someone to ask us to sing duets in church. In any case, before we were school age, the two of us stood in front of the whole congregation (with more than a little fear) to sing together. We were guided by our mother who taught us new songs and coached us in notes, pronunciation, and proper public behavior. Nor were we the only children to sing for the congregation. Sibling groups or sometimes whole families provided special worship music.

was the center of our home. My mother played for church services and improvised beautifully. She created an invitation to sing—the atmosphere in our home was that you sing wholeheartedly and that you sing with energy and enthusiasm because that is what the music is calling for. One of my earliest memories is of my sister and me sitting on our living room floor looking up at grown men singing. My father's male quartet was practicing with my mother—they sang gospel songs and just loved it! When we got together with our extended family, the ten of us cousins would sing—folk songs, lots of fun songs, and then we would also sing from the hymnal.[16]

A young man remembered, "The important thing about worship was being there singing hymns with my family. Even when I couldn't read the music or the words, I would stand up on the bench and help them hold the hymn book and just sing along. To me that was a very special time."

The song often remembered as the first one learned was the German hymn "Gott ist die Liebe" (No. 167). Even though very few of those interviewed grew up speaking German, this hymn held a special place in many hearts and linked them with an important piece of their people's tradition. One called the song a lullaby; another recalled that her father always chose this hymn when he played the piano at home, and that in his last years as his dementia deepened, this was the hymn he still tried to play.

"I learned to sing when I was afraid," World War II refugee Justina Neufeld said. Her earliest memories of singing were connected with long, cold evenings when the house was darkened so marauding Russian soldiers would not find them. With her mother and aunt, she sang "Wehrlos und verlassen" ("In the rifted Rock I'm resting," No. 526) very softly and felt God's comfort. Later on the trek out of Russia, she and other refugees would sit in the dark (because a fire would have given away their location), tell stories, and sing songs of heaven.[17]

Learning how to sing melodies and harmony parts was an important experience for many. Since Old Mennonite churches typically did not allow musical instruments in worship until the 1960s, most people said they learned to sing simply by listening to other voices. One woman recalled, "My dad would put me on his lap and hold my face and say, 'Sing like I do,' and that's how I learned to sing alto." Another woman remembered everybody singing as they did the dishes. "The older ones would try to teach me to harmonize as soon as I could—first of all, to hold the melody while they harmonized around me," she said. "It was essentially the extracurricular activity of the family."

A man remembered that his father didn't sing very much, so he sat beside his mother in church to "absorb her alto" and learn to sing parts. Another man recalled sitting beside his dad at singing school and learning to sing tenor. Still another said:

> My parents were surprised when, before I learned to read, I began singing a part just from listening to our records. I didn't know I was doing anything unusual—I sang both the melody and tenor lines of "There is a balm in Gilead" (No. 627).[18]

Relatives—aunts in particular, it seems—were important in passing on the singing tradition. A woman recalled, "I remember singing even before I learned to read words—watching the book and just dying to know. An aunt pointed out the words and music line to me. I think I was singing harmony by second grade."
Another person recalled:

> My aunties, whom I got to sit with in church, were very good singers. They were altos and could sing with vibrato—and this was exciting! They taught me very many things. Because I was short, I used to watch their tummies, and I could see the way they breathed; they said you had to breathe there in the middle and not up at the top. They also instructed me that when you sing, you pronounce the words differently. If you speak, you say *path*, but when you sing, you say *pahth*. I was very open to their instruction.[19]

Joetta Handrich Schlabach had a precise memory of learning to sing harmony.

> It is like asking me, "Where were you when President Kennedy was killed?" Although learning to read music and hear harmonies

was a progressive, multifaceted event influenced by taking piano lessons and growing up with four-part singing in the church, I have a vivid memory of the day when I actually sang alto for the first time. I believe I was nine or ten when my mother and I made a ten-hour trip to pick up my brother from college. During the long hours we sang, and at some point she taught me the alto line for "The old rugged cross." Once I had it down, she switched to soprano and we sang a duet. I'm not especially fond of that song today, but I value it as my entree to harmonization.

The hard work of harmony continued, sometimes in strange and humorous ways. My two older sisters and I shared a bedroom. Some nights before going to sleep, my musically gifted older sister would try to get us to sing like the White Sisters, whose religious recordings we had. We were never quite as successful as they, but we usually fell asleep as tired from laughing at our failed attempts as from the day's activities. Our favorite song was "It's not an easy road"—a fitting metaphor for the hard but enjoyable work of learning to make music together.[20]

In the memories of those interviewed, an important element of the tradition was that *anyone* could participate in singing. "I never had the feeling that I had to be very good in order to participate," one said. "It was just something everybody did." Another person commented, "There was a real sense of belonging and having something you could contribute. Two of my brothers and sisters were adopted cousins; though they didn't have a musical bent and couldn't keep a tune, they were always with us in our music making."

An actor, who said he didn't consider himself a great singer, described how he experiences singing in the congregation:

When you see yourself as a member of a cast as in a theater performance and you are giving yourself to the production rather than seeing how well you can do, you become an important cog in a bigger piece. I feel best about singing in a group when I don't worry about how I'm doing or whether the person in front of me is assessing all my mistakes. Maybe it's in losing yourself that you gain more for yourself because in the act, as acting is, it's a selfless experience. But it's not effortless for me, so I find myself struggling sometimes in hymn singing. But when I don't, that's when I feel connectedness to the group.[21]

A traditional way children as well as adults were taught to sing was in singing schools and regular gatherings for singing. One interviewee had written a poem as a teenager about S. G. Shetler, a singing school instructor who traveled all the way from Pennsylvania to Oregon to give singing instruction. Several of the lines were:

> Where he stores all his knowledge we cannot tell.
> It surely is there we know quite well. . . .
> He's teaching music to each boy and girl.
> With sharps and flats our heads are a-whirl.[22]

An older interviewee remembered a "Mr. Shoemaker" who came to the church every year and taught children to read notes (but not shaped notes, as would have been the case in her parents' generation).[23] Another remembered a man who came every week during winter months to teach the *do-re-mi* method and the thrill of "suddenly being able to understand and sing and make music and harmony with other people." Many others remembered ad hoc ensembles or youth groups singing together simply for fun. One person described a quaint dating custom in which couples who double-dated would "sing those Stamps-Baxter songs for fun just as fast as we could." Such innocent goings-on seem long ago and far away; one man commented with regret that today his children seem to sing more as an academic exercise than for fun:

> Singing is just another competition. For me, singing was a delight—a game, fun. Now young people think singing always has to be very good. If it isn't "1" quality, they don't feel comfortable. They may be learning to sing as well as my generation did, but they don't enjoy singing as much because it's work.[24]

Leading the Community's Song

Other memories of singing included the first experience of leading a song. One person recalled how leaders were initiated in his congregation:

> We distributed *The Way* [an evangelistic leaflet] once a month. Before we went out, we gathered [at the church], sat down on the benches, and talked about what routes we were going to take, and

before we went, we had a song and prayer. That was normally where you led your first song.

Another way we broke new song leaders in was to have an experienced song leader open a worship service with two hymns; then after the scripture reading, the inexperienced person would lead a song with the support of the congregation, who had already warmed up their voices.[25]

One woman recalled that in her congregation, young women could lead singing for Sunday school but were not permitted to do so in the worship service until they were married. Others remembered that women were *never* allowed to lead singing in worship, only in Sunday school. One woman said that she began to lead congregational singing as a freshman in high school. When asked how she was trained for the role, she said, "We learned just by watching what happened. The singing schools had a lot to do with it too, giving us security with music and enjoying it."

Another described how her father came to lead singing:

My father was in some kind of a band and played guitar and loved to sing the popular music of the day. Then when he was converted, he gave himself and his music making totally to the church. And I think because he had a wonderful tenor voice, he naturally led with his voice. I assume that over a period of time he just learned the church music and learned to conduct. He was very astute at observing and learning that way, and I think that's just simply what he did. He was a wonderful natural musician, and any time he didn't get it, my mother would keep him in line because she knew how to count and knew how things would go. They would practice till he got it.[26]

As part of the horizontal connection created by singing, many of those interviewed could remember specific song leaders—their personalities, styles of directing, and their particular role in worship. In defining a good song leader, one said simply, "They are able to help you see the song by what they do." Another said of a remembered song leader, "I could tell that Clarence Rich loved music as much as I did, and that made me want to sing." Another spoke appreciatively of song leaders who recognize that when a song leads people to holy ground, "you don't want to quick move to something else, you just sort of soak a little, sustain it a little." In describing the basic habits of an effective song leader, one person mentioned "enthusiasm, good facial expression, and thorough preparation. The leader needs to understand the different meters and be able to beat out the time correctly with the hand. The leader also needs to pitch the song correctly and start the song with vigor."

As he spoke about what makes a good song leader, evangelist George R. Brunk II told about his brother, the song leader at many of the revival meetings he held:

> Lawrence had a charisma about him. He nearly always talked about a song, something that he thought would be of interest to the people, and he was able to stimulate them into a mood for singing. After he started it off, which was the main thing he did, they took it away. He was not a trained song leader, didn't know much about songs, but his voice—he had a bass voice, and he could get people to sing.
>
> My first requirement [of a song leader] is animation. I find a dead song leader hard to endure. Some of them are very mechanical in their time beats. Just lately, I worked on some of our young fellas—I said, "Get your hand up there." The other night we had a song service, and someone called on me. I'd never led a song in our church, so I got up and tried to demonstrate what I think they ought to try to do—the beat, some art, or whatever you call it. They believed me, they sat there with a joy. Visualize me leading a song![27]

Another person said:

> I think a well-led hymn—whether it's led from the keyboard or by directing—takes into account the music and the text and what the hymn writer might have been wanting to convey. You have a sense where the leader is going. When they first raise their arm, we know that this is going to be a little more meditative or it's going to be a little more joyful and full of praise. So before you start, you've got in your own mind what this hymn is all about.[28]

Eleanor Kreider, a long-time mission worker in England, described her own song leading habits:

In England, we're in a society where people are used to being led by the organ, which means there is no human face in front of the congregation. What I like to do is to get up and teach people a song. I like to read it, and I find it makes a tremendous difference in how they are able to sing it—the role of the human, the leader. There is a kind of impersonality about hymn singing if it is led by an unseen instrument up in the gallery. The shaman, the person of spirit, is leading in their face and in their voice—and it isn't just the tempo or the pitch.[29]

One person acknowledged that though every song leader may do things from time to time that irritate the congregation, people "will tolerate an awful lot if they trust you." Noting that certain leaders are simply better accepted by a congregation, he said,

Michael [Bishop] can seem to get away with things that other people can't. I think part of it is because he's like that all the time—he is what he is all the time. He's short, he's energetic, and people seem to accept that in him. When he leads, his love of music is just oozing out of him so much that you can forgive him anything he could do, even if it was something you hated.[30]

One song leader confessed that it is distracting to sing with other leaders if they don't have the "feel" of the song or go too fast or too slow. Another reflected theologically on the fact that not everyone has the potential to become a song leader.

How do you deal with the fact that the church is the priesthood of all believers, a place where people should be allowed to use their gifts and to develop their gifts? That is something I believe in. At the same time, for music to go well, you need people who know how to play and who spend time at this and who are good at this. . . . If we're going to practice the priesthood of all believers, we have to realize that we are not all priests in the same way, that there are still different needs and different gifts.[31]

The people who were interviewed were not too shy to complain about incompetent or ineffective song leaders. In fact, it was clear that the horizontal connections created by singing can be damaged by leaders who lack skill.

Some of my most disappointing Sunday mornings have to do with a mediocre song leader. Someone who didn't prepare adequately ahead of time. Someone who looks in the book instead of making eye contact with the congregation. Someone who doesn't give us time to breathe between stanzas. . . . If it's a hymn or song that we're using with guitars, you do the work ahead of time to figure it out with your accompanist. The sense of "Oh well, this thing'll get off the ground eventually" doesn't do it. [The song leader needs] a sense of confidence: "I'm comfortable doing this, and you will be able to sing this the same way." When a song leader is not confident, that's exactly how the congregation will sing. It's best then too when the song leader knows the bigger picture of the morning: How is this hymn functioning here? Why did this one get put here? And then of course, you hope they will understand the purpose and focus of worship, too.[32]

Another said:

What really distracts is lack of preparation, especially for new worship leaders. They don't really understand what all it involves. They just think we stand up there and sing, and it's not that easy. [They need] to get beyond the technical aspect and to at least have the look that they are very comfortable with doing it. I think the worship leader really has to focus if he or she is there to lead worship. They have to do their work ahead of time. Eye contact and body language can say a lot to invite people or put up barriers.[33]

And still another:

Some song leaders make me feel like I'm being dragged or jerked around. I don't like that. I need a little bit of pause before I go to that second verse. Don't punish or scold the people you are leading. Sometimes this happens with adults in a more subtle way [when song leaders imply by their actions]: "I'm going to make it very obvious that you are going slow. I'm really going to make you breathless." That is also a form of scolding.[34]

In effect, those we interviewed were describing in effective song leaders a *priestly* role—the skill not only to embody the song and lead it well but the ability to open a way into God's presence.

Making Harmony

Magic is what we do. Music is the way we do it.
—Jerry Garcia[35]

Singing together is clearly an act of relationship—women and men, old and young, leader and people. But the deep bonds that are formed have even more significance. What Mennonites told us is that the body of Christ is created as we sing together. Some called what happens "magic"—the amazing harmony and unity that come to be because of a song.

In one person's imagination, singing together requires the cooperative spirit of dancing:

> On Sunday morning there was the beginning "folk dance" of everyone getting there. We would sing until everyone got into their places—gathering songs, the gospel songs. There were always three songs at the beginning and usually one before the sermon, sometimes one at the end. When we sang, there was a certain exhilaration. Singing gave us a way to get beyond some of the problems that divided our congregation.[36]

To sense the spirit of harmony in the midst of singing expands the experience. "I know that everybody is with a hymn, with the music, because the women are listening to the men," one person said. "We are listening to each other, and that makes me shiver when that happens."

What is amazing and mysterious is that even as unity is created, the individual remains complete and whole. Describing this paradox, a woman remembered what happened in worship during the weeks that her father awaited death:

> While our family was preparing ourselves and Dad was preparing himself for death, there was this interactive kind of thing going on in Sunday worship that was very important to me. The congregation had no idea what I was hearing in those songs. Sometimes I was singing and sometimes not singing but entering into another dimension of life and death. The songs we sang helped me move through that process.[37]

Another person who moved from the West Coast to the East Coast, leaving family and church behind, said:

> On those last Sundays I couldn't sing. I'd open up the hymnal for the first hymn of the morning and I'd get two words out, and that was it! On the last Sunday I remember thinking that this was the last sermon I would hear here. That didn't bother me, but I couldn't sing. I couldn't sing even one word of a song.[38]

Mennonites know well the vulnerability and depth of community that is created by singing together. Though this powerful gift can be taken for granted, it can also spring up to surprise us when we least expect it. One such occasion, as recalled by Goshen (Indiana) College president Shirley Showalter, was at the annual faculty conference at Eastern Mennonite University, where she was the guest speaker and where professor Barbra Graber was leading the faculty in an old-fashioned, call-out-the-number hymn sing:

> Someone requested "Thuma mina" (No. 434), which Barb said she did not know. She asked for help. "Blow the pitch," someone said. So she blew the pitch on her pitch pipe, and then someone started to sing. A few people, without prompting, sang the opening solo line, and then the whole group followed, singing in full, joyful harmony.
>
> When I approached the podium, I said, "I hope you noticed what happened here already this morning. All Barb had to do was blow the pitch, and immediately there was music. Some of you sang the solo parts. The rest of us found the other notes. Something much bigger than any single one of us created itself in front of us."
>
> This moment is symbolic, touching a long history in which music has provided a way of building Christian community and creating a worshipful center through which the Spirit of God enters into our midst, penetrating body, mind, and heart.[39]

Another person summarized how this mysterious unity works: "Singing undresses us. When we sing, we bring our bodies into the room, and our souls are undressed. I have this image of all these souls speaking to each other and then real things starting to happen."

The love of singing among Mennonites springs from deep wells of faith nurtured in both the family and the congregation where singing functions as an ordinary, everyday way of communing with God as well as an expression of the community's love of unity and harmony with each other. One man observed that in a cappella singing, Mennonites create an image of themselves as they most want to be and which they hope to sustain throughout the week: a people in love with God and with each other.

Singing Unveils an Inner Landscape

Although it was relatively easy for Mennonites to talk about what happens on a human or temporal or horizontal level when they sing, it was far more difficult for many of those interviewed to tell us what happens between them and God. Often they stumbled for words, searching for ways to express the inexpressible. Yet what was abundantly clear is that meeting God is the heart of the matter. On their way to talking about how singing connects them with God, Mennonites often reflected first on the powerful emotional territory created by song.

By culture, Mennonites are a reserved, unexpressive people. We are reluctant to reveal deep feelings. We would rather show our love for others by building barns or feeding the hungry. Yet our faith is profoundly important to us, and when we sing, we discover deep wells of desire for God's presence and love. One person we interviewed observed:

> We Mennonites are considerably more comfortable expressing our piety when we sing than in any other form. We are not nearly as free when we pray out loud in a group, and we certainly are not willing to be as pious in our language in a discussion or a sermon. Though we sing, "Open the wells of grace and salvation,"[40] we don't talk that way when we are talking about our faith or about the sermon. But we are willing to sing using that kind of language.[41]

Singing gives Mennonites permission to get in touch with their own human feelings as well as feelings directed to God. "Music cre-

514 Lord, I am fondly, earnestly

OPEN THE WELLS 10 9. 10 9 with refrain

1 Lord, I am fond - ly, ear - nest - ly long - ing in - to thy
2 Dead to the world would I be, O Fa - ther, dead un - to
3 I would be thine, and serve thee for - ev - er, filled with thy

ho - ly like - ness to grow, thirst - ing for more and deep - er com-
sin, a - live un - to thee. Cru - ci - fy all the earth - ly with-
Spir - it, lost in thy love. Come to my heart, Lord, come with a -

Refrain

mun - ion, yearn - ing thy love more ful - ly to know.
in me, emp - tied of sin and self may I be.
noint - ing, show - ers of grace send down from a - bove. O - pen the

wells of grace and sal - va - tion, pour the rich
O - pen the wells of grace and sal - va - tion,

Text: Elisha A. Hoffman, *Church and Sunday School Hymnal*, 1902
Music: Charles E. Pollack, *Church and Sunday School Hymnal*, 1902

streams   deep   in - to my   heart. Cleanse and re - fine   my
pour the rich streams deep in - to my heart.   Cleanse and re-fine my

thought and af-fec-tion, seal me and make   me   pure as thou   art.
thought and af-fec-tion,   seal me and make me pure as thou   art.

ates some kind of opening—a sense of freedom," one person told us. Another person said, "Songs give me permission to be fervent." A young man acknowledged that it wasn't until he tried to sing at a friend's father's funeral that he even recognized his grief. "I had been so caught up in thinking that I didn't realize I had emotions," he said. "And then in the hymns, I lost it. I actually recognized what emotions were there and that I needed to start feeling them."

One man confessed, "With many hymns, I'm wiping tears." He noted that the power of hymns to awaken feelings affects even those who can't or don't sing. "My wife says her dad didn't particularly sing, but he would wipe tears from his eyes when he heard singing—this big farmer, you know," he said. Another person said that it wasn't until she moved away from her home congregation that she recognized the powerful emotional impact of singing together in worship. "For almost a year [afterward] I was unable to sing in church without crying," she said.

Not every powerful emotion generated by music was positive, however. Many, many of those interviewed complained about negative emotions connected with altar calls. One person remembered:

I hated singing with invitations [altar calls]. I just felt like I was never going to get out of that church alive! We were going to die and go to hell as sure as could be. I don't like to hear those songs to this day. They're so foreign to what I think about God. I don't think of God as being something that should scare me. I want to think of a God of love.[42]

Another person confessed, "To this day on those rare occasions when 'Just as I am, without one plea' (No. 516) is sung in a worship service, I have to fight. I don't want to sing it. I don't want to hear it. I'm serious. I still ask myself, 'Am I going to hell?' "

What people most detested was the feeling of being manipulated by that particular song. "I think I wasn't really a bad person, and I had probably gone forward before," one said. "But when that song was sung I thought there ought to be something [bad] I needed to dredge up." Another said, "I remember thinking it was kind of dumb and that I felt used in some way. I think I was especially angry when the evangelist said this would be the last song or the last verse, and then he didn't keep his word, and we kept on singing."

Yet another person said:

I don't like to sing "Just as I am" because I felt coerced by that hymn too often. Nobody else was coming forward and to make the evangelist feel better, I felt maybe I should do it one more time. Even as a child, I thought I should always come, so I went forward at least a dozen times. I was embarrassed then, and my mother was embarrassed, and so I don't want to sing that song. Luckily, I haven't run into that one for quite a while.[43]

On a positive side, a number of people told stories of how a particular song at a particular time expressed their deepest emotions and provided a welcome release. In explaining this phenomenon, song writer Chuck Neufeld noted that good hymns "tell our story; they don't just tell the song writer's story."

A woman told how comforting it had been to sing with the congregation after a fellow church member, a mother in her forties, was tragically killed in an auto accident. "We had a special service on that Sunday morning," she said. "The pastor talked about what had happened and chose hymns that allowed us to express what we were feeling—the shock and pain."

People marveled at the capacity of a song to perfectly connect with and express the emotional and spiritual textures of an experience. A pastor commented:

> Sometimes I plan worship and things really click and connect for people. At other times none of that happens. I don't get real upset because I guess you have to strike out once in a while, like in baseball. On the Sunday after our organist discovered she had cancer, my wife led "Precious Lord, take my hand" (No. 575), which I had chosen because I felt it was an appropriate response to the sermon, but it ended up that because of this particular event in this family's life, it was a very moving experience for many, many people in the congregation. I've never had so many people tell me they were moved to tears by the singing of a hymn. It just seemed it was the right time for it.[44]

Singing Reveals a Path to God

Though not all emotions people feel can be construed as a response to God, Mennonites tend to label the emotions that hymns produce as communication coming from God or as a response to God. Perhaps what is happening is that these emotions open up an otherwise closed channel of awareness—and in the context of hymn singing, that openness is directed to God.

The Mennonites that we interviewed were especially conscious of the power of poetic hymn texts to usher them into sacred territory. One person told us the first hymn she remembers singing is an old gospel song, "The love of God is greater far" (No. 538, *Mennonite Hymnal*). She recalled:

> My father loved that song, and I loved the imagery in it—an ocean of ink, skies of parchment, every stalk on earth a quill, every man a scribe, draining the ocean dry to write the love of God. I just had a lot of fun sitting in church pondering that image.[45]

Several people mentioned "Lord, should rising whirlwinds" (No. 92), also known as the second half of the hymn-poem "Praise to God, immortal praise" (No. 91). For one person who had encountered poverty and war first hand, the song spoke assurance that "in the middle of all this enormous pain and suffering and deprivation

538 THE LOVE OF GOD

LOVE OF GOD 8.8.8.8.8.8.6.8.6. with Refrain

F. M. Lehman, c. 1917

F. M. Lehman, c. 1917
Arranged by Claudia Lehman Mays

1 The love of God is great-er far Than tongue or pen can ev - er tell;
2 When hoar - y time shall pass a - way, And earth-ly thrones and king-doms fall;
3 Could we with ink the o - cean fill And were the skies of parch-ment made;

It goes be-yond the high - est star, And reach-es to the low - est hell.
When men who here re-fuse to pray, On rocks and hills and moun-tains call;
Were ev - ery stalk on earth a quill, And ev - ery man a scribe by trade;

The guilt - y pair, bowed down with care, God gave His Son to win;
God's love, so sure, shall still en - dure, All meas - ure - less and strong;
To write the love of God a - bove Would drain the o - cean dry;

His err - ing child He rec - on - ciled, And par - doned from his sin.
Re - deem - ing grace to Ad - am's race The saints' and an - gels' song.
Nor could the scroll con - tain the whole, Though stretched from sky to sky.

REFRAIN

O love of God, how rich and pure! How meas - ure - less and strong!

It shall for - ev - er-more en - dure The saints' and an - gels' song.

that is mostly caused by human beings, God is still present with us." Another commented, "I never sing that song without being aware of the storm imagery and remembering how God promises not to destroy people. Hymn texts have a lot to do with the way I perceive God."

Of course, not every musical setting proves worthy of the text assigned to it. "Because I like poetry, I must confess that a lot of poetry gets punished by the music to which it is set," one person lamented.

But when images are apt and the music is worthy, a hymn can provoke continuous and ongoing reflection. One person quoted the line "Here in this world, dying and living, we are each other's bread and wine" from "What is this place" (No. 1) and said this image would sustain for weeks, months, and years to come—indeed, for a lifetime.

The biblical image of God as sheltering rock in the refrain of "A wonderful Savior is Jesus" (No. 598) appealed to several people. One said:

> I think the poetry is just wonderful—"He hideth my soul in the cleft of the rock, where rivers of pleasure I see." I spent time at Joshua Tree National Monument, a desert place in California. When you've been out in the sun, the cleft of a rock is the most wonderful place. You find this little place in the rock where you can get away from the sun, and it's cool and you can get into the rock and cuddle up and get relief from the sun.[46]

Many of those interviewed were aware that sacred biblical texts have become a treasured part of their experience through song: for example, certain psalms, a gospel story, or scripture texts in classic works such as *Messiah*. A woman remembered the exhilaration of, as a child, joining the adult choir on Palm Sunday to sing "The Palms" and the convergence of her world and the world of scripture.

> Recreating the Bible story of Jesus coming into Jerusalem along with the singing of music that somebody else had written that was now coming to life here, and adults were doing it and we were doing it with them, and it was all very wonderful, very grand. The

music of Palm Sunday drew me into the story as well as into this moment of music making and worship.[47]

It is not surprising that a familiarity with biblical and poetic texts in song also forms the theology of those who sing. Both theology in the abstract as well as functional theology—the beliefs that shape people's everyday experience of God—are often derived from the songs they sing. Hymn texts are quoted in daily life with the same practical authority as scripture; they are used to comfort, to explain God's ways, or to affirm one's faith. Some people quote William Cowper's line "God moves in a mysterious way his wonders to perform" (from No. 80, *Mennonite Hymnal*) when faced with perplexing or surprising circumstances. As a personal testimony, people have been known to use "I know whom I have believed, and am persuaded that He is able to keep that which I've committed unto Him against that day," part of "I know not why God's wondrous grace" (No. 338).

Beyond providing a foundation for belief, the vision of God that emerges from song also powerfully shapes people's personal experience of the divine. One person said, "The upbeat, happy rhythms of gospel songs—'To God be the glory' (No. 102), 'Praise him, praise him, Jesus our blessed Redeemer' (No. 100)—assure me of God's power and might." Another person said, "In the hymn 'Holy, holy, holy!' (No. 120), I sing to a holy, righteous, powerful God—a Spirit who is present. 'In the rifted Rock I'm resting' (No. 526) reveals a God who created the world, sustains it, and will win in the long run."

In addition to images of God as powerful and mighty, hymns also brought singers face to face with a tender, compassionate God. "When we sing, I can sometimes almost see God in a white robe at the cross in front of the church with outstretched, welcoming hands," one man said. Marlene remembers how these lines from "My Shepherd will supply my need" (No. 589)

> *There would I find a settled rest,*
> *while others go and come,*
> *no more a stranger, nor a guest,*
> *but like a child at home.*

permanently altered her childhood image of a strict, unrelenting God-as-judge to one of God as a fundamentally loving parent. This transforming revelation opened the way for other refreshing and renewing images to come.

A number of women commented on how important it has been to find images of a feminine God revealed in hymns such as "Mothering God, you gave me birth" (No. 482) and "O God, great womb" (No. 155). One woman remembered the warm images of God in "Children of the heavenly Father" (No. 616):

> I remember singing and loving this hymn as a child—I thought it was a children's hymn and claimed it as my own. It seemed to be a balm for the loneliness I experienced as a ten-to-thirteen-year-old missionary kid away from home in boarding school.
>
> But years later when my father died, I found new truths and meaning in it and now consider it a most powerful reminder of God's protecting and loving care. The simplicity of the melody, rhythm, and supporting harmony seem to be such an integral part of the whole hymn, supporting the warm and strong text.[48]

Through singing, the finitude of human creatures in God's presence impressed another:

> When I sing, I confess that I am a creature before my Creator. I am nudged. I am held. I am invited to bring the stuff from my week, the small stuff. I bring that—that's who I am as I sing and pray. But the singing and praying move me beyond that. I see a bigger picture than this little piece I bring.[49]

Such self-knowledge may not always be welcome. One person acknowledged that "sometimes people don't allow themselves to be open during singing—it's a kind of fear of being vulnerable to God and to the Holy Spirit dealing with us, revealing areas in our lives for which we may need to ask forgiveness."

A young man told a story of being ambushed by a song as he sat in church one morning. For some time he had been intending to talk to his pastor about being baptized but just kept putting it off. He had gone through the baptism preparation classes twice before and both times decided he wasn't ready for baptism. Now, as a twenty-year-old, he was seriously considering Christ's call in his life.

One Sunday morning during the prayers of intercession, his congregation sang "Lord, listen to your children" (No. 353). After singing it several times, they hummed it over and over while the pastor prayed. The man said:

> I'll never forget the sound of that humming—the most beautiful sound over and over again. I just started to cry. It was the best cry I ever had. I confessed my sins to God, and I decided I do want to be baptized. Then I decided to think about it for a week before telling anyone because I wanted to be sure it wasn't just something emotional. A week later, I decided it was for real.[50]

Even as people struggled to define the capacity of singing to connect them with spiritual reality, the interviews pushed them to try to describe what music alone—separate from text—can do to connect them with God. They provided a variety of descriptions:

"Music makes the words speak a little louder."

"Music helps me remember the text. It connects inside me better than the text alone does. It enhances, sort of solidifies the text."

"If someone reads a scripture in worship that has been set to music—for example a *Messiah* or *Holy City* text, it's much more meaningful to me to have the two things together in my mind. Without music, the reading is flat."

"The text doesn't really matter that much. Sometimes we sing texts we disagree with or don't like. Music makes a connection that lasts—the beauty of it."

"The importance of words is that they are only there as a vehicle to connect with the whole body experience."

"Music moves the story along."

"The music gives the text color, a human emotional dimension to the words."

"When we sing, we say the words much more slowly. As mind and spirit interact with the music, there may be twenty or thirty possible meanings to a phrase. Certain musical sequences do something inside me—some are a call to prayer, some a call to repentance or a call to thanks. The music feels that way—I can't explain why."

"There is something which is beyond words. Probably just as profound as music is silence. When I go on retreat, I struggle with words. I'm not always very good with words, and I prefer being free from that sometimes. Maybe that's one of the reasons I concentrate more on the music than on the words of hymns. Words don't open up in the same way as music does. Especially poetry in hymns. Watts really gets us into the framework. This is theology that we're singing. It's like being in a conversation with somebody who talks a lot. It's kind of difficult to engage them in a discussion! There's not much room to disagree with Watts. You can disagree with him, but then what do you do?"

Several people attempted to describe what the music of a particular song contributed to its meaning. Sometimes the *sound* of a song created or called forth a particular response to God:

"The Taizé song 'Veni Sancte Spiritus' (No. 298) is so simple and repetitive with beautiful harmony. The repetition provides stability, an undergirding."[51]

"I could just say the words of 'I owe the Lord a morning song' (No. 651), and they would be meaningful, but the song isn't complete without the music. It's the joy—it does something to my spirit."

"There's something about the refrain of 'My life flows on' (No. 580) that as I sing it, I really feel no storm can shake me. The music feels really solid and true."

Other people found congruence between the sound of a song and a particular dimension of God's character:

"In the old German hymn 'Gott ist die Liebe' (No. 167), I sense God's love in the incredible gentle and playful sound that the music communicates."

" 'There's a wideness in God's mercy' (No. 145) is an absolutely first-rate combination of text and music where the text is talking about breadth, and there's very broad, expansive music. It just goes on as long as you can produce tone. It's like the music becomes a metaphor for the limited metaphor of the text."

Jean Janzen reflected on what happens to poetry when a musical setting is chosen:

In the combination of words and music, the words are strengthened by rhythm and voice. The music itself echoes the words. When a poem is read [aloud], someone puts emphasis on the words and slows down where they want to. With music, you go the next step. You set it to tone, you set those words even more dramatically in the direction the composer wants to go so that your rhythms and the emphases—your high notes—are placed on certain words. It can work two ways: it can limit the text, or it can make it larger. When a poem is set to music, in a way it's bound— like being cast in bronze instead of letting the bronze be molten. But the beauty can be expressed in that form. . . . When you look at a sculpture, it can become many things. It can expand. For example, with my poem "Mothering God" (No. 482), the sustained E pitch [gives] an intensity to the text that was almost a cry—a cry of longing. I realized that this text is a really strong appeal—probably different from what I felt [when I wrote it]. The music [by Janet Peachey] is certainly powerful.[52]

Michael Bishop, a song leader, admitted,

I don't care how beautiful the text is, if the music isn't right for it, if it is not achievable and magical for the congregation to be able to taste it and feel it, the text doesn't get through. It might be a beautiful text, but the music didn't provide the necessary transportation. I think they are equal, but one is more equal than the other.[53]

Singing Becomes Our Best Way to Pray

Beyond creating understanding and belief, singing is a gateway to prayer for Mennonites. Other traditions have their own prompts for prayer: icons or incense or stained glass windows or silence or the Eucharist or the words of a prayer book. For Mennonites the prompt for prayer is singing, and we pray best when we sing.

Many—though not all interviewees—said that they are praying when they are singing. As a child put it, "I try to mean the words I sing—I just kind of sing it to God." Another person reflected:

Learning to pray by myself as a youngster was something that was not natural. I'm not sure we really teach children to pray. But I just sort of stumbled onto hymns as a way to pray. I remember

Prayer is the soul's sincere desire 572

DORKING CM

1 Prayer is the soul's sin - cere de - sire,
2 Prayer is the bur - den of a sigh,
3 Prayer is the sim - plest form of speech
4 Prayer is the Chris - tian's vi - tal breath,
5 O Christ, by whom we come to God,

1 un - utter - ed or ex - pressed, the mo - tion of a
2 the fall - ing of a tear, the up - ward glanc - ing
3 that in - fant lips can try; prayer the sub - lim - est
4 the Chris - tian's na - tive air, the watch-word at the
5 the life, the truth, the way; the path of prayer that

1 hid - den fire that trem - bles in the breast.
2 of an eye, when none but God is near.
3 strains that reach the Ma - jes - ty on high.
4 gates of death while en - t'ring heav'n with prayer.
5 you have trod, Lord, teach us how to pray.

Text: James Montgomery, 1818, alt.
Music: Stephanie Martin, 1990
Copyright © 1990 Stephanie Martin, 990 Glencairn Ave., Toronto, ON M6B 2A9. Used by permission.

going through the hymn book when I was quite young and coming to "The old rugged cross." I remember crying and crying. Somehow it touched me as I sang and played alone. It's not a song I would choose now, but at the moment, it gave me a way to pray.[54]

One person said, "Singing is almost *always* praying. We are communicating with God with word and sound. It's the easiest way to pray. The Spirit expresses for us what we can't find words for." Another said:

It has occurred to me that the verse about "pray without ceasing" may be stating a fact, not a commandment. What we dwell on and what we think about expands, and it becomes our prayer whether we decide it will or not. How we connect with another human being is our prayer; our life is a prayer; we are either full of prayers that condemn us to worry and fear, or we are filling our lives with prayers that enrich us. Singing is probably closer to prayer than most words ever get.[55]

Another person said, "A song is often a prayer that can't be prayed or that needs to be prayed when I can't pray. For me it is that prayer that doesn't end, so in some ways when I do music, I feel like I am obeying the scripture to pray without ceasing."

A man who thinks of prayer as dialogue explained:

If prayer is maintaining some kind of openness to God, then that dialogue—whether articulate or inarticulate—that flows between me and God is prayer. In much of my hymn singing, that dialogue is certainly there. So yes, often when I am singing, I am praying— even if the song is not a prayer text as such.[56]

"The songs rise up when I need them—the ones that speak about the struggle of the journey and the strength that comes from centering in God," a woman said. "I often find myself singing them as a prayer."

Another woman was also sure that singing is a form of prayer. "The words are what is meaningful to me, but the music carries them and makes them real," she said. "I even change the words of songs sometimes—I change *us* and *we* to *I* because that's exactly how I feel as I sing between me and the Lord."

For some, the connection between prayer and singing easily occurred during personal prayer. One person said she sang inward tunes, like the songs of Taizé, during her times of personal prayer; another also mentioned beginning her daily prayer and meditation with Taizé songs. "These songs help me focus and don't bombard me with excess theology," she said.

One person admitted:

I have a difficult time practicing personal spiritual disciplines regularly. I often think I will [practice them]—so I buy a special book or decide upon a special place to go and get a candle to burn, but lo and behold, a couple of weeks later I've abandoned my plan.

One regular practice at which I do succeed, however, is simply to pick up my hymnal and start looking through it for hymns I enjoy and sing them to myself. This may not actually count as a discipline because it takes no self-discipline to do it—it is something that comes up out of me. It's a need. I may have other more pressing things to do, but when I see my hymnal lying there, the next thing I know I've spent forty-five minutes thumbing through it singing to myself and God.

If I sing a new song I like in corporate worship, then that song is one I must look up and add to my repertoire of favorites. Usually when I find a new song I like, I live with it for a couple of weeks—singing it often. I have also committed some or all of the stanzas of my favorite hymns to memory so I can sing them while driving.[57]

A young adult told how prayer happened best for her as she played hymns on the piano and sang them: "I experienced God in a different way than in times of scripture reading and [verbal] prayer. I often longed for that time alone with God—whether I was sad or joyful, just anytime."

Another version of the story of "hymn book as prayer book" came from eastern Pennsylvania:

I do not think either side of my family was very gifted musically and certainly not well-trained. I grew up without benefit of piano or any other musical instrument until in tenth grade when I bought an old piano and taught myself to play. Most of what I heard at home were the songs of my mother's youth—"Clementine," "Darling Nellie Gray," and the 33–r.p.m. records of gospel songs about a railroad to heaven and a cabin in the corner of glory land.

But then there was church and a Mennonite grade school where I was introduced to the hymns of the church. And unexpectedly, my home became a place to learn those hymns—word by word and note by note.

Blame it on the chickens. The eggs they produced were our livelihood, and it was my detested chore from the ages of eight to fourteen to grade the eggs on our electric grader in the shanty next to our house. Each day from Tuesday to Saturday there were five baskets of eggs to grade and box—and ten baskets on Monday. I wore down my school friends' patience by constant complaints about my miserable lot in life.

My only consolation was the old black 1927 *Church Hymnal.* Each day I propped it next to the ramp on which I placed the eggs. Starting with "Come, Thou Almighty King" on page one, I would sing my way through the hymnal. And for an hour or two each afternoon, the flutter of "angels bending near the earth" would transform the ugly little shanty into a holy place.

This was no skip-around, sing-the-first-line endeavor. I memorized every verse of every song I knew, unless it was a tune I truly disliked. I learned the shapes of all the notes in our shaped-note hymnal and would sometimes sing the alto as a change from the melody line. The words [and music] of the hymns sank deep into my soul, even as a preteen—from Isaac Watts and J. S. Bach to Ira Sankey and Fannie Crosby.

My only departures from this regular routine came at Christmas and Easter, when I gave myself up to the celebration at hand. The images burned themselves into my brain: "glories streaming from heaven afar" at Christmas, the measured Good Friday march to "the judgment hall" to "view the Lord of life arraigned," the Easter "Hail him!" following "the faithful women weeping" before they knew "the stone was rolled away." Whenever the calendar ran out before the hymns were all sung at church, I finished them in the shanty.

Singing in church or school as I grew older, I barely needed a hymnal. How could all these people stand there with their noses in the book? Wasn't it intuitively obvious which verse came next? Lift up your heads, you fellow saints, and let it roll out![58]

A man reported that he sings scripture, such as psalms, aloud to spontaneously composed tunes. The same thing happens as he prays with his own words: "Early in the morning I may take a walk in the park and instead of saying a prayer, I'll sing my prayer."

An exercise enthusiast told of his own personal formula for praying and running:

> I sometimes tell people, "I teach for a living, but I run for my life." When I run, I not only get bodily exercise, I also worship—often in song. My lungs are otherwise engaged, so I do not sing with my voice. I sing in my spirit. One of the songs which often comes to mind and spirit while my feet hit the pavement is "Joyful, joyful we adore thee" (No. 71). The 2/2 meter of this hymn tune resonates well with the steady rhythm of my foot beats. I have to admit that I make some adjustments in the rhythm in order to accommodate my running style: I insert quarter notes where the tune calls for the dotted quarter followed by an eighth note. My "singing" of this hymn leads me to claim that indeed bodily exercise does profit, especially when combined with spiritual exercise![59]

Even those people who had trouble with traditional definitions of prayer could connect with the idea of singing as prayer. One person confessed:

> I've never understood the power of traditional prayer—bowing my head and saying words, coming up with the right phrase. That doesn't do anything for me compared with singing. I find prayer in that sense happening all the time in all kinds of ways. Sometimes it's the four parts that get you in that space [of prayer]; there are just more possibilities with music.[60]

Another person responded, "I guess you know *prayer* is one of those words that has baggage for me. But if I would describe prayer as sort of two-way communication, it definitely feels like when I'm singing I'm plugged in, and it's going both ways." Still another person said, "It seems I've lost most of my piety [over the years], but it's in singing hymns that I feel like I experience what piety tries to do—establish a relationship with God."

When we pressed people further to talk about what happens in prayer as they sing, two kinds of responses emerged. People spoke of singing as a form of prayerful supplication to God. For example, one person said, "The songs that move me are the ones that are pleas to Jesus." People also described experiences of praise-filled prayer that could only be expressed in song, as illustrated by this story:

> Several hundred people had gathered in an open-air style courtyard of a convention center. Most were seated in the lower level; the rest of us were seated on the next-higher level on three sides. Above us, hotel guests leaned on the balcony railing watching what was happening below.
>
> Our song leader . . . opened the evening with "Day is dying in the west" (No. 493, *Mennonite Hymnal*). Soft music rose from the lower level like a warm, misty fog. While we sang "Day is dying in the west, heaven is touching earth with rest," we couldn't see it happening outside, but we knew it was.
>
> Harmony woven together with unity reached me with "Wait and worship while the night sets her evening lamps alight through all the sky." Again we couldn't see it happening outside, but we knew it was.
>
> "Holy, holy, holy, Lord God of hosts!" The whole atmosphere seemed charged with the presence of God. "Heaven and earth are full of thee." The whole congregation's voice began its crescendo as we ended with "Heaven and earth are praising thee, O Lord, most high."
>
> I forgot about the people watching on the balcony. I forgot about the people seated around me. All I can remember is . . . entering into the most perfect praise I knew how to do.[61]

Another memory of music as both solemn and filled with joy comes from a foot washing service, held twice a year in traditional Mennonite communities.

> It was a high occasion, and the music that was sung was not sung at other times of the year. Preceding communion, the ritual of the council meeting had quite a bit of terror and fear in it. Ministers called the members of the congregation to account. My memories are that it was really sort of scary and solemn. . . with extremes of emotion, the searching for sin and being willing to confess. You daren't lie and say you are ready to take communion if you aren't!
>
> Once that was over and the people passed, then we could have communion. Children didn't get grape juice and bread—only the baptized members, so we got baptized fairly young. . . .
>
> At communion there was a sense of transcending individuality

. . . . The ritual made everybody feel like one organism in a way that was not usual on Sunday mornings. The men sat on one side and the women on the other. During foot washing the men pulled up their trouser legs and pulled off their socks, and we [children] saw their calloused bunion feet. Uncle Orval would bang the pitchfork, get his pitch with his nasal voice, hum the tune, and we would all sing. When he would go to wash feet, another uncle would lead the singing. People would call out favorite songs—it was freer as the foot washing got under way.

At the beginning of the service, the singing would have been subdued, quiet and serious, but with beautiful harmony. Toward the end everything got messier with people walking in and out of the anteroom, men putting their socks back up, women fixing their coverings and strings and capes and garters. It got more boisterous and lighter, more festive and celebrative. We sang Easter songs, "Low in the grave he lay" (No. 273) and the three-page "Easter Anthem" (No. 613, *Mennonite Hymnal*). It was exhilarating because that was the only time of year we sang [these songs].[62]

A Kansas woman also described the relationship between singing and praise:

The God I am aware of as I sing is one who loves beauty, the Creator of all things beautiful. Yesterday morning I went to the library at 9 a.m. to catch up on some tasks before the library opens at 10. When it was getting close to 10 and things still needed to be done, I walked to the east door to unlock it. Across the street is a large, gold-colored maple tree. Behind it next to the brick building is a fiery red bush, and there was a Bradford pear with leaves that were red at the top and green at the bottom, and there were other gold-colored trees. It was just so beautiful. And that's when I should have stepped out into the street and sung—no matter what—"Let the whole creation cry" (No. 51).[63]

Singing Heals and Transforms

The power of music to fortify or strengthen people when they felt weak, discouraged, or afraid was amply documented in the interviews. In times of fear, people found courage in singing; in times of uncertainty, people discovered they could trust; in times of pain, people found comfort and healing. What happens when people sing

God of grace and God of glory 366

CWM RHONDDA 87. 87. 87 extended

1 God of grace and God of glo - ry, on thy peo - ple
2 Lo! the hosts of e - vil round us scorn thy Christ, as -
3 Cure thy chil - dren's war - ring mad - ness; bend our pride to
4 Save us from weak res - ig - na - tion to the e - vils

pour thy pow'r. Crown thine an - cient church's sto - ry, bring her
sail his ways! From the fears that long have bound us, free our
thy con - trol. Shame our wan - ton, self - ish glad - ness, rich in
we de - plore. Let the search for thy sal - va - tion be our

bud to glo - rious flow'r. Grant us wis - dom, grant us cour - age,
hearts to faith and praise. Grant us wis - dom, grant us cour - age,
things and poor in soul. Grant us wis - dom, grant us cour - age,
glo - ry ev - er - more. Grant us wis - dom, grant us cour - age,

for the fac - ing of this hour, for the fac - ing of this hour.
for the liv - ing of these days, for the liv - ing of these days.
lest we miss thy king - dom's goal, lest we miss thy king - dom's goal.
serv - ing thee whom we a - dore, serv - ing thee whom we a - dore.

Text: Harry E. Fosdick, 1930, *Praise and Service*, 1932
Music: John Hughes, 1905 or 1907, *The Voice of Thanksgiving, No. 4*, 1928

goes beyond the immediate moment and even changes the shape and direction of their lives.

Two people brought us stories of critical moments when the extraordinary power of "God of grace and God of glory" (No. 366) met their need. One person recalled a story told by Harry Martens, a legendary fund raiser for Associated Mennonite Biblical Seminary. Martens had gone to Bangladesh to do famine relief. Entirely overwhelmed by the level of need, he went out one day in a taxi to try to find a church. When he passed a church where they were singing "God of grace and God of glory," he went inside and found what he needed to continue his work. The hymn renewed his strength and his trust in God.

John Paul Lederach, an international peace negotiator and a professor at Eastern Mennonite University, also remembered the power of this hymn.

> My story involves Harry Emerson Fosdick—a theologian, preacher 9/11/2001
> and author. Here was a person who had the nerve to say, in the
> midst of World War II, "This is a great time to be alive." Here was
> a man who spoke out against the war perpetuated by all sides and
> who wrote, "Our problem is not to see how little we can believe
> but what great things we can see in the Christian message and
> make real to the world that desperately needs them. This is a great
> time for great convictions."
>
> Fosdick also penned the occasional words to hymns. One of
> those entered my life and has found a way to weave its rhythms
> and words through my experience of God. In 1930, between the
> great wars of this century, Fosdick, at the age of fifty-two, wrote
> the words to "God of grace and God of glory." I remember singing
> this song as a child, though it was not until I was in high school
> that the words leapt out and grabbed my conscience. This may
> have partly been due to the influence of my dad (John Lederach)
> and my uncle (Ron Kennel), who had shared the hobby of collect-
> ing the writings and books of Harry Emerson Fosdick. I remember
> them saying, here by my paraphrase, "This may be the greatest
> song in our hymnal."
>
> The words are simple rhymes:
>
> *God of grace and God of glory,*
> *on thy people pour thy pow'r.*

Crown thine ancient church's story,
bring her bud to glorious flow'r.

Lo! the hosts of evil round us
scorn thy Christ, assail his ways!
From the fears that long have bound us,
free our hearts to faith and praise.

Cure thy children's warring madness;
bend our pride to thy control.
Shame our wanton, selfish gladness,
rich in things and poor in soul.

Save us from weak resignation
to the evils we deplore.
Let the search for thy salvation
be our glory evermore.

The chorus brings forward the phrase, "Grant us wisdom, grant us courage, for the facing of this hour, for the living of these days." I always imagined Fosdick writing these words with the context of the Great War behind him and the prospects of the next about to happen. But I had no idea how deeply the song had been engrained in my own psyche until I was walking the mucky soils of war and violence in Central America.

It is not an easy story to tell, but a short version starts with my involvement in a Mennonite Central Committee assignment. As part of my work in providing resources for conflict transformation and peace building in the region, I became involved in supporting the peace process and negotiations in Nicaragua taking place between the east coast indigenous resistance . . . and the Sandinista government.

Those of us involved in this mediation effort, most of whom were religious leaders from Nicaragua, found that as we made progress in establishing negotiations, we also made enemies and came under considerable pressure to stop our work. At times the pressure took the form of simple messages and cynicism about whether the effort would succeed. At other times it was much greater.

In my case, my family and I were located in San José, Costa Rica, and I was the one member of the team who had a passport that permitted me to travel at a moment's notice between Indian leaders located in Costa Rica and the Sandinista government in Managua. At certain points in the process, I became the key shuttle. I can remember that we held regular meetings of the Indian leaders in our home in San José. And then I would travel up to Managua to carry their messages and bring back the government's response. As might be suspected, I came under pressure since I was seen as a key communication link in the process.

The first real sign of serious pressure came when we were advised of a plan to kidnap our daughter Angie, a story that is far too complex to relate here. The plan was put in motion by a series of characters involved with and operating under the Ollie North network. . . . On receiving notification of the plans, we moved the family out of Costa Rica, and I continued to work on the negotiation process, traveling back and forth without a home base.

The second major point of pressure came about a month later when I was informed that a contract had been taken out on my life. It was a little disconcerting to know that I was not worth more than a couple of hundred dollars, although when we first heard it we thought the whole thing sounded preposterous. Threats had come and gone, so we kept working, even though I began to take more precautions. Then, just days later, I was arrested by Costa Rican immigration officials on returning from Nicaragua to San José. It happened to be the day when then-President Oscar Arias was in Norway and Sweden receiving his Nobel Peace Prize for setting in motion the Central American peace accords, and half of his government was with him. The progressive half. The other half, or at least some elements of them who were paid [by] and connected to the CIA, were feeling their oats. Let me say this was not one of my more delightful days or nights, and it included such interesting features as mug shots, accusations of drug trafficking, and charges of falsifying official documents. They seemed to have more information on me than I had about myself, and I watched them shuttle copies of my documents to a black-windowed limousine outside their office. My captors were quite insistent that I was Colombian and connected to a five hundred–kilo cocaine shipment. At the end of a long day and well into the late hours of the night, I was finally deposited—after a dizzying ride in a nonlicensed vehicle in the back streets of San José—at a local hotel.

By morning I was joined by several members of the Conciliation Team who had traveled from Nicaragua. We were meeting in the hotel room to decide what we should do next when I was called out of that meeting and went with one of my Nicaraguan colleagues to the hotel lobby. There two east coast resistance members informed us that the assassination plot was on. Visibly shaken and nervous, they absolutely insisted there was a contract on my head. They had specific details: two men were in that very hotel that morning trying to establish a way that I could be identified so the contract could be carried out. They argued forcefully that I should get out as soon as possible.

A few minutes later, on leaving the hotel, I was visited in an extraordinary way by the God of grace and the God of glory. I must confess that by this time I was so frightened I was sweating straight out of my palms. It is amazing what fear and paranoia can do to your mind. I found my eyes darting around and looking into every face as if it might be the assassin. I could not get my heart to slow down, and my stomach felt like a raw pit. They had gotten to me. I was flat-out scared.

What I remember is that Faroan Dometz, a Moravian pastor and fellow member of our mediation team, and I left the hotel to go across town and retrieve some personal belongings and documents from another office. We set out in the late afternoon and walked for some time in silence. Then Faroan said to me, "I am very afraid for you and your family." We walked again in silence. I remember my head being too full even to think. Thoughts ran every direction and banged into each other.

Then out of the blue, without saying a word, Faroan started to whistle "God of grace and God of glory," by Harry Emerson Fosdick. We had never talked about that song. He had no idea what it meant for me. He whistled it the whole way to the office. It was as if the air he blew through his lips was the very breath of God blowing on my face.[64]

Another time in people's lives when songs brought strength and comfort was at the time of death. Jean Janzen remembered joining her sister to sing songs her mother loved at her mother's deathbed—and her mother, even though she was very weak, making a trio from her bed. She also recalled that not every hymn seemed appropriate at such a time.

For some reason my sister would ask me if the songs were okay to sing. One was "All the way my Savior leads me" (No. 573, *Mennonite Hymnal*). I said, "Well, sure." We sang about half a dozen songs, and then she asked about "Take time to be holy" (No. 177,

Life Songs No. 2). "Is this all right?" And I surprised myself by saying, "No, I don't want to sing that." She started laughing, and then we both started laughing. She was finally able to say, "Why don't you want to sing it?" I said, "It's because it's so heavy. I can't imagine singing all that piety, especially when someone is at the end of their life. Are you going to lay all of this on them?" And then I remembered I never did like that song very much:

> *Take time to be holy,*
> *speak oft with thy Lord.*
> *Abide in him always,*
> *and feed on his word.*
> *Make friends with God's children,*
> *help those who are weak . . .*

and something else yet. How many things can you do in one verse—that's only one verse of the hymn! I mean, how much piety can you layer on one fragile soul!

We laughed so hard the nurse finally came in to see if we were crying because we were wiping our eyes. My sister said she doesn't think she will ever sing that song again.[65]

There were several stories of people in the last stages of illness who were able to sing even after they were no longer able to speak. One person remembered:

Our family's custom was to sing together on Sunday evenings after the evening service—the last thing we did before we started a new week. It was often a sad time because it was the end of the weekend. The last time I visited my mother when she was still living, she was in a nursing home and she couldn't speak at all, couldn't move—there wasn't much left of her. My dad said to all of us, "Let's sing together." I thought, "Oh no, how am I going to get through this?" He brought out a stack of books, and we sang all the songs we could remember that mom would have liked. I tried to stay intellectual and cynical so I could get through it, and oh boy—here comes this song about heaven and harps and all this. But my mother sang along through part of it! That was something: she didn't speak, but she sang.[66]

A nurse in Mountain Lake, Minnesota, who works in an Alzheimer's unit told us that the patients there often become agitated and cannot be comforted. She has learned to walk up beside them and sing a hymn. When she does, they become quiet and contented.

Twila K. Yoder wrote of how, on his deathbed, her brother reached for a song to express his love for God.

> In February 1995, my brother, Marlin, whose eyesight and rich tenor voice had been robbed by AIDS, lay dying in a hospice center in Indianapolis. Along with his battle with this dreaded disease, the previous years had been marked by a valiant spiritual quest that brought him to a place of inner peace and genuine knowledge of the love of God. Music had been at the center of his life for many years. Just a few days before he died, no longer able to sing, he haltingly spoke the words of every verse and every refrain of "How great Thou art" (No. 535, *Mennonite Hymnal*). These words, now etched on the stone that marks his grave, are forever etched in my heart as a reminder of the tremendous love of God that evokes such wonder and praise.[67]

Another moving story of music and healing was told by George Brunk III, dean of Eastern Mennonite Seminary, who reflected on the great solace and encouragement he found in particular texts and music as he battled spinal meningitis. Through two surgeries and many months of recuperation, he became more deeply aware of the power of song to mediate God's restoring strength:

> Providentially, in the weeks immediately preceding my illness, I had been listening to Mendelssohn's *Elijah* and practicing the choruses in preparation for the annual [Shenandoah Valley] Bach Festival. This music and the texts coursed through my mind during those agonizing hours of pain, uncertainty, and fear. "He shall give his angels charge over thee, that they shall protect thee in all the ways thou goest."
>
> In the lonely hours of sleeplessness: "He watching over Israel slumbers not nor sleeps." What if I am left an invalid or my family must go on without me? "Cast thy burden upon the Lord and he shall sustain thee" (No. 586). How long can this ordeal last? "O rest in the Lord." Do I have the strength to see it through? "Lift thine eyes, O lift thine eyes to the mountains, whence cometh help. Thy help cometh from the Lord, the maker of heaven and earth." What a lesson in preparation for the inevitable crises of life![68]

Even though people may be formed in sturdy faith, their life experiences can damage their trust in God and their confidence in life. Eleanor Kreider told a story of the power of music and a supportive community to restore her to health after great grief:

> When I was in my twenties, I went through very, very deep waters. My husband died, and then my child died. I felt like I had hit bottom. At the time I was directing a choir at church, which sang from the balcony. Choir members met just before each service to learn new music so we could lead and support the congregation. That choir was so good to me. When it came time to sing in the service, I would start to cry, and I would cry continuously. They just allowed that. They didn't say, "Well, pull yourself together, and when you get over your grief, then come and direct the choir." They didn't say that. They allowed it. For a whole year they allowed me to grieve, and I always look back on that as a time of great healing for me—such a gift from those people.[69]

Another story told of healing from depression:

> During my college years I began suffering from depression (although I didn't realize that was what it was at the time). Mild depression stayed with me for more than ten years. During some of the darker moments, singing hymns—both alone and at church—was my primary therapy. Lyrics and music together simultaneously echoed my pain, allowing the tears to flow, and provided words for a confession of faith when I didn't feel like I was standing on a very firm foundation. I sang my way through the pain of two miscarriages, through my questions of faith, through some of the painful memories of growing up, and through my uncertainty about where God was leading me. It didn't seem to matter much from whence came the pain; the same hymns could touch the inner chords and bring much release: "O Thou, in whose presence" (No. 559), "What wondrous love is this" (No. 530), "Thou true Vine, that heals the nations" (No. 373), "God is here among us" (No. 16), "O Splendor of God's glory bright" (No. 646), "My Shepherd will supply my need" (No. 589), "Father eternal, Ruler of creation" (No. 447, *Mennonite Hymnal*), "Come, O thou Traveler" (No. 503), and "In the stillness of the evening" (No. 551). Even though these were often alone and lonely times, each hymn represented the faith community, faith passed down, and I was reminded of the cloud of witnesses.

Somewhere toward the end of this weekend [church music] conference, I realized that my depression is truly over. I've been feeling progressively better for the last several years, but all at once the reality hit me: I'd been spending the entire weekend wrapped in hymn singing, and it hadn't touched the tender areas that used to bring tears so easily. Tears came several times, usually in response to the speaker's stories or poems, but the emotion I felt was the pain of someone else, not my own.

An unusual story of the healing power of song was told to us by Philadelphia poet Jeanne Murray Walker about friends of her family:

A couple who had a son wanted a second child but had difficulty conceiving. When they finally became pregnant a second time, they were concerned that their five-year-old son might feel displaced by the new baby. They developed a bed-time ritual in which the child would sing to his little sister in the womb, "You are my sunshine, my only sunshine. . . ." Each day the child sang his song.

When the little sister was born, she was very ill. She was placed in isolation, where her tiny body was hooked to many wires and tubes in hopes of saving her life. Her parents stayed with her at the hospital while their son, unable to see his sister, remained at home with a sitter.

The baby did not get better. In fact, the doctors told her parents that she could not be expected to live. The father decided that if this was to be so, there could be no harm in bringing his son, with his germs, to see his sister. So when the nurses left the isolation room, he dressed his son in the requisite hospital garb and smuggled him into the baby's room.

After observing his sister for a few moments, the little boy began singing, "You are my sunshine, my only sunshine. . . ." At the sound of his singing, she opened her eyes, and from then on began to get better. Today the child is a thriving, healthy two-year-old.[70]

That music may, in fact, be medicine was the topic of a Sunday morning sermon preached by Jennie Knoop, who punctuated the sermon with the remarkable refrain, "We are resonant beings, and music is our medicine." These, in part, are the words she delivered to the 1994 Unitarian-Universalist Musicians Network Conference at The Mountain in Highlands, North Carolina:

I'm going to speak to you this morning about the power of music to heal. The word *heal* comes from the same word as *whole* or *health*. Healing does not always mean *curing*. A person may be healed without being freed from a disease, just as a person may be cured of a disease and still be in need of healing.

Healing restores the deepest balance within each of us. Healing returns us to the place where we are at home in the universe, confident in ourselves and life, restored to the interdependent web. It should not surprise you to learn that one of the greatest healing forces known to us is music.

About twenty years ago in Durham, North Carolina, I went to my first black gospel concert. I noticed there was someone nervously following the soloist around, someone with a towel over one arm. I wondered why there seemed to be so many nurses standing around. Well, the room heated up with each song. The power of song and rhythm was unbelievable. It felt like a huge heart beating. I took my pulse and the pulses of everybody around me who would let me. Each heart was beating right in time to the music.

We were unified and we were inspired, transfused, and lifted out of ourselves. Down front people were falling out left and right. "Falling out" is an experience of surrender that is spiritual, emotional, and physical, an experience of release that, I am convinced, is deeply cathartic and therapeutic.

I think we all recognize the way music touches us deeply. It stirs us, opens us, brings tears to our eyes. It sends energy flowing in chills and waves from our heads to our toes. Music can also enlarge us, lift us up, and open the wings of our souls.[71]

For one woman we interviewed, an old gospel hymn became a testimony of healing after the trauma of sexual abuse was confronted in her family. She told of choosing to sing "When peace, like a river" (No. 336) at her wedding. Though she had needed to stay away from her family for at least two difficult, fragile years, they were reunited at her wedding. And even though not all the healing was complete, they were able to sing the lines:

> *My sin* [meaning her family's sin]—*not in part, but the whole*—
> *is nailed to his cross, and I bear it no more,*
> *praise the Lord, praise the Lord, O my soul!*

She said it was "a mountainous sort of accomplishment."

Healing through song happens not only for individuals but for families and communities. A woman told of her family's despair when a daughter ran away. "Sometimes during sleepless nights, my husband and I would walk down the country miles, stop and hold each other and cry," she said. "And then we'd pray. What else could we do? Where else could we turn?" Thirty-five years later, the daughter is an advanced alcoholic. The woman said, "Again and again we find 'the peace of Christ makes fresh my heart'—words from my favorite hymn, 'My life flows on' (No. 580). Though I cannot carry a tune, I have memorized hundreds of hymns. How they bless me as I pray, meditate, walk, or go about my tasks."

That same hymn took on unusual significance for many people at Associated Mennonite Biblical Seminary, who recalled how important it had been for the community to sing together during the days and weeks after President Marlin Miller's unexpected death in early November 1994. At the chapel service on the morning following his death, the community was stunned with grief. When they sang the refrain of "My life flows on,"

> *No storm can shake my inmost calm*
> *while to that Rock I'm clinging.*
> *Since love is Lord of heav'n and earth,*
> *how can I keep from singing?*

it was as though they clung to the music for their very life and breath. After thirty days of mourning, they gathered again in the chapel and attempted to sing the hymn. This time many found they could not sing the song. Now past the initial bewilderment and overwhelmed by the intensity of their loss, they had no breath for the song's affirmation. Yet the song was there, and they could trust that someday they would be able to sing it again.

Throughout our interviews, people spoke of finding themselves profoundly restored to relationships in the midst of singing—their relationship with God, with others, themselves. Words like *renewal*, *comfort*, and *peace* were never far from their lips. But something more also emerged from their stories. People described an energy

that surged from singing and a vision for the future that transformed their lives.

One person talked about "the freshness that comes over me in
singing." Another simply used the word *challenge* to describe the
effect of particular songs. One person said, "Music connects us
with God and God's energy in a way that very few other things do."

One woman had a vivid memory from her teen years in Holland
just after World War II. She described attending a once-a-month
evening worship service in a large old Lutheran church in Amster-
dam (across from the Mennonite church, *Singelkirk*) with her Girl
Scout group. All the scouts marched in together singing a hymn to
the tune of "I sing the mighty power of God" (but with slightly different words than the American version, which is No. 46): "The
kingdom you established on earth is being attacked from all sides
by the enemies of the light." It went on to call them to be
"guardians of the gates." She said:

> When these one thousand teenagers sang this hymn with the ac-
> companiment of the large pipe organ, I felt the roof would fly off
> the building. I recall being filled with zeal and fervor that together
> we could and would make this a better world.[72]

For another woman, singing was both a political act in the midst
of present realities and an expression of hope in God's ultimate
reign of justice and peace:

> Music making is so many things: it's the eschatological thing—
> joining the heavenly choir, joining that eternal praise. In the face of
> a world that's willing to blow itself up, what is a faithful response?
> Well, to sing and dance! Singing hymns is a political kind of act
> because it says who is in control. And I'm not![73]

With abundant power to transform both inner and outer reality,
singing is indeed a wondrous gift to worshipers—whether in the
worldwide church at worship, in the local church family gathered
on Sunday, or in the worship that occurs in solitude. Music brings
comfort, healing, peace, joy, and delight; it also probes, convicts,
and propels us to action. What happens when Mennonites sing is

far more complex than anyone would ever dream—our music is intertwined with the very fiber of our faith and, in the image of George Herbert, it is "thy silk twist let down from heav'n to me [to] both conduct and teach me, how by it to climbe to Thee."

I can't imagine anything
but music that could have
brought about this alchemy.
Maybe it's because music is
about as physical as it gets:
your essential rhythm is your
heartbeat; your essential
sound, the breath. We're
walking temples of noise,
and when you add tender
hearts to this mix, it somehow
lets us meet in places we
couldn't get to any other way.

—*Anne Lamott*[1]

Part Three

Toward a Spirituality of Song

Come, O Creator Spirit, come   27

VENI CREATOR SPIRITUS LM

1 Come, O Cre - a - tor   Spir - it, come,   and make with - in   our
2 O   Com - fort - er, that   name is thine,   of   God most high the
3 Our sens - es   with thy   light in - flame,   our hearts to heav'n - ly
4 May we   by   thee the   Fa - ther learn,   and know the Son, and

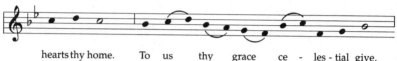

hearts thy home.   To   us   thy   grace   ce - les - tial give,
gift   di - vine;   the well   of   life,   the   fire of love,
love   re - claim,   our bod - ies'   poor   in - fir - mi - ty
thee   dis - cern,   who art   of   both,   and   so   a - dore

who   of   thy   breath - ing   move and live.
our   souls' a - noint - ing   from   a - bove.
with   strength per - pet - ual   for - ti - fy.
in   per - fect   faith for -   ev - er - more.   A - men

Text: anonymous, *Veni Creator Spiritus*, 9th century; tr. Robert Bridges, *Yattendon Hymnal*, 1899
Music: anonymous, Plainsong, 4th c.

Postmodern Spiritual Landscapes

At the beginning of the twenty-first century, the Western world finds itself in the midst of an ongoing spiritual revolution. In her book, *A History of God*, Karen Armstrong observes that our era is the only age in history that has not regarded some form of faith as natural and normative.[2] Yet in ways no one could have predicted, the most secular people in the history of the world have become eager to engage the world of the spirit. Eugene Peterson, pastor-turned-professor, looks at this development with a somewhat skeptical eye:

> Overnight spirituality has become a passion for millions of North Americans. It should be no surprise [though] that a people so badly trained in intimacy and transcendence might not do too well in their quest. Most anything at hand that gives a feeling of closeness—whether genitals or cocaine—will do for intimacy. And most anything exotic that induces a sense of mystery—from mantras to river rafting—will do for transcendence.[3]

Nor has this quest for spiritual reality bypassed the church. Reflecting on his encounters with evangelicals, Roman Catholic Henri Nouwen said:

> I love the directness [of evangelicals], speaking about Jesus without embarrassment or complications, [but they have] a great need for a mystical dimension to their lives so they could be more free in living and not driven. The question is not, "How many people did I bring to Jesus?" but "How faithful has your life with Jesus been?"[4]

Another way of asking Nouwen's question is: How vital is our connection with God? How are we nourishing the spiritual roots of our lives? Whether secular or religious, many postmodern North Americans cannot satisfactorily answer questions on the spirit side of the ledger. Instead, a vibrant, soul-satisfying faith seems just beyond our reach.

One way people throughout history have found their faith renewed is in the sacraments of the church—those gifts of God that bring life, health, and joy to the people of God. Because the Mennonite Church had its origins in a quarrel over sacraments (and thus tended to downplay the role of sacraments), the sacraments have not been highly regarded as key elements in spiritual formation. The church has depended on the preached and taught Word of God, along with daily discipleship, to communicate and nourish faith.

Though the traditional modes of Anabaptist spiritual formation—preaching, teaching, and modeling—are extremely valuable and were largely sufficient in a time when communal bonds were strong, they no longer suffice in a world of powerful secular influences. Deeply affected by rationalism, fundamentalism, or social activism, preaching and teaching in mid- to late-twentieth-century practice have sometimes lacked spiritual depth or warmth. In many places, frequent gatherings of a close-knit community of faith have diminished to one-hour Sunday morning events that leave little opportunity for the mentoring and modeling that were important elements of nurture in the past. The deforming influences of secularism have considerably weakened the faith and commitments of many in the church. In a time when people seek direct experience of the spiritual world, some have left their congregations in search of spiritual vitality elsewhere. Others have simply drifted away and succumbed to the lure of materialism and secularism.

Although churches have offered a variety of responses to this dilemma, one thing is essential: Vital worship that speaks to and calls forth responses from both mind and heart is required. Whether that style of worship leans toward the charismatic or the liturgical or some other flavor does not seem nearly as significant as whether it reunites the separated head and heart. What the interviews in this project have shown is that hymn singing is the one sure way such integration happens for Mennonites. If faith is to grow and thrive in our congregations, people need to sing.

What is interesting to observe, however, is the growing awareness in the larger culture of the significant role of music in spiritual formation. Mennonites are certainly not alone in their experience and understanding of the power of song. Several widely read contemporary authors share the conviction that music is essential in their spiritual journey. In *The Cloister Walk*, Kathleen Norris reflects on the role of song in her return to Christian faith. Participating in Benedictine liturgy one day, she heard a call to conversion in the scripture reading.

When I first heard [the words from Revelation] in the monks' choir, tears welled up in me, unexpected and unwelcome. I remembered how completely I had loved God, and church, as a child, and how easily I had drifted away as a young adult.

I realized suddenly that I'd been most fortunate in being given another chance to encounter worship, in middle age, in a context that restored to me the true religion of my childhood, which was song. For me, participating in monastic lectio has meant rediscovering a religion that consists not so much of ideas or doctrines but of song and breath.[5]

Anne Lamott describes how church singing lured her away from a colorful weekend flea market near Sausolito, California, that she used to visit on Sunday mornings.

If I happened to be there between eleven and one on Sundays, I could hear gospel music coming from a church right across the street. It was called St. Andrew Presbyterian, and it looked homely and impoverished, a ramshackle building with a cross on top, sitting on a small parcel of land with a few skinny pine trees. But the music wafting out was so pretty that I would stop and listen. I knew a lot of the hymns from the times I'd gone to church with my grandparents and from the albums we'd had of spirituals. Finally, I began stopping in at St. Andrew from time to time, standing in the doorway to listen to the songs. I couldn't believe how run-down it was, with terrible linoleum that was brown and overshined, and plastic stained-glass windows. But it had a choir of five black women and one rather Amish-looking white man making all that glorious noise, and a congregation of thirty people or so, radiating kindness and warmth. During the time when people hugged and greeted each other, various people would come back to where I stood to shake my hand or try to hug me; I was as frozen and stiff as Richard Nixon. After this, Scripture was read, and then the minister . . . would preach . . . and it would be . . .

enough to send me running back to the sanctuary of the flea market. . . .

I went back to St. Andrew about once a month. No one tried to con me into sitting down or staying. I always left before the sermon. I loved singing, even about Jesus, but I just didn't want to be preached at about him. To me, Jesus made about as much sense as Scientology or dowsing. But the church smelled wonderful, like the air had nourishment in it, or like it was composed of these people's exhalations, of warmth and faith and peace. There were always children running around or being embraced . . . and every other week they brought huge tubs of great food for the homeless families living at the shelter near the canal to the north. I loved this. But it was the singing that pulled me in and split me wide open.

I could sing better here than I ever had before. As part of these people, even though I stayed in the doorway, I did not recognize my voice or know where it was coming from, but sometimes I felt like I could sing forever.

Eventually, a few months after I started coming, I took a seat in one of the folding chairs, off by myself. Then the singing enveloped me. It was furry and resonant, coming from everyone's very heart. There was no sense of performance or judgment, only that the music was breath and food.

Something inside me that was stiff and rotting would feel soft and tender. Somehow the singing wore down all the boundaries and distinctions that kept me so isolated. Sitting there, standing with them to sing, sometimes so shaky and sick that I felt like I might tip over, I felt bigger than myself, like I was being taken care of, tricked into coming back to life. But I had to leave before the sermon.[6]

Sam Keen, who once called himself Christian but now feels more comfortable identifying himself as an agnostic, writes:

I can't go back to traditional religion. Neither can I live within the smog-bound horizon of the secular-progressive faith. So I search for a way to unite the demands of the head and heart. Without falling into mindless faith or surrendering to authority, I want to find a way to lean on the everlasting arms. . . .

The truth of the spirit, as I know it, is better conveyed in song and poetry than by propositions. The best of the Christian tradition, which continues to nourish me, is expressed in the music it inspired. Often, my mind is uncomforted by any set of beliefs that can stand the test of doubt, but when I listen to Bach's "Sheep May Safely Graze," my soul lies down beside still waters and a mysterious Lord is still my shepherd.

The journey we are undertaking must contain a melodic element. We need to heed the advice of Socrates' daemon who advised that the practice of philosophy without musical accompaniment is hazardous to the soul. There is something essentially musical about the Western spiritual path.[7]

Even those who identify themselves as atheists recognize the splendor and captivating power of religious music. One such choral singer reflected on the dilemma he faces at Easter, when his thoughts turn to Bach's *St. Matthew's Passion*:

What if the religious sentiment in the *St. Matthew* leaves you cold? Does the music become less involving, and therefore less moving? The problem for the nonbeliever is not the music itself—far from it. Sound impinges on the sensory organs of atheist and believer in precisely the same way, and the physiological response to melody, harmony, and dynamics is probably similar.

In a sense, the text doesn't matter; music is a language in its own right and one which is not easily pressed into communicating specifics. It addresses the emotions (or, for the believer, the spirit) in ways which stir the deepest yearnings and the highest aspirations of atheist and believer alike.[8]

What Kathleen Norris, Anne Lamott, Sam Keen, and other postmodern folk have in common is a worldview that requires a moving personal encounter with the world of spirit in order for belief to be possible. Why does music bring one to such an encounter? What is it about music that opens the doorway to the divine?

In his book *Faithquakes*, Leonard Sweet, former chancellor of United Theological Seminary in Dayton, Ohio, asserts that "music is the means to God for much of postmodern culture." He goes on to explain how people in the industrial era lost their voices—and ultimately their souls—to machines. The world tours of pop stars like Garth Brooks and Madonna show that music is in itself a spiritual experience—whether that music happens inside or outside the church. Sweet suggests that group singing and communal musical experience are the chief community-building forces of the postmodern era. With power to move people beyond themselves, music is a key to recovering the soul.

> Music is an absolute imperative if postmoderns are to move outside of themselves, connect with others, and build community. One can motivate and move individuals to an experience of God without music—perhaps. But to have a community experience of God's presence, to bring a community of faith to a "catalytic moment," . . . music is a must.[9]

Directions from Scripture and the Church

Such an appreciation for the critical relationship between faith and song does not belong only to the modern or postmodern era. From ancient times, music and spiritual experience have been intimately connected. Since the earliest days of the Christian church, singing has held a revered role in worship. A familiar portion of Paul's letter to the Christians at Colossae, for example, encourages believers to sing.

> Let the word of Christ dwell in you richly; teach and admonish one another in all wisdom; and with gratitude in your hearts sing psalms, hymns, and spiritual songs to God.[10]

Other biblical texts speak of music as part of personal or group worship. Luke's gospel contains the Magnificat, Mary's remarkable hymn of praise and a vision of God's reign of peace and justice. Both Matthew and Mark mention that just before Jesus went to the Garden of Gethsemane on the night before he died, he sang a hymn with his disciples. The vision of John on the island of Patmos includes thousands upon thousands of singers and choirs who participate in the fulfillment of Christ's reign. More than once, choirs from every tribe, language, and nation are joined by angelic hosts who offer songs of praise and glory to the Lamb.

In the fifth century, Augustine (who included singing in his list of sacraments[11]) extolled the power of singing to encourage and bring joy.

On the happiness of the heavenly alleluia, sung in security, in fear of no adversity! We shall have no enemies in heaven, we shall never lose a friend. God's praises are sung both there and here, but here they are sung in anxiety, there, in security; here they are sung by those destined to die, there, by those destined to live forever; here they are sung in hope, there, in hope's fulfillment; here they are sung by wayfarers, there, by those living in their own country.

So let us sing now, not in order to enjoy a life of leisure, but in order to lighten our labors. You should sing as wayfarers do—sing, but continue your journey. Do not be lazy, but sing to make your journey more enjoyable. Sing, but keep going.[12]

Theophan, an Orthodox Christian of the eighth century, not only encouraged Christians to sing but suggested that the act of singing is directly linked with the Holy Spirit's action in the believer.

"Speaking to yourselves in psalms and hymns and spiritual songs, singing and making melody in your heart to the Lord." [Ephesians 5:19]

How should we interpret these words? Do they mean that when you are filled with the Spirit, you should then sing with your mouth and your heart? Or that if you wish to be filled with the Holy Spirit, you should first sing? Is the singing with mouth and heart, mentioned by the apostle, meant to be the consequence of being filled by the Spirit, or the means towards it?

The infusion of the Holy Spirit does not lie within our power. It comes as the Spirit wishes. And when it comes, this infusion will so greatly animate the powers of our spirit that the song to God breaks out of itself. Freedom of choice lies only between leaving this song to be sung in the heart alone, or expressing it aloud for all to hear.

The words of the apostle must be taken in the second sense rather than the first. Desire to be filled with the Spirit, and sing with that aim in mind. Singing will set alight the Spirit.[13]

Protestant reformer Martin Luther, a lover of music and composer of hymns, also held singing in high esteem.

I am not satisfied with those who despise music, as all fanatics do, for music is an endowment and a gift of God, not a gift of other persons. It also drives away the devil and makes people cheerful;

one forgets all anger, unchasteness, pride, and other vices. I place music next to theology and give it the highest praise.[14]

On their way to persecution and death, the early Anabaptists sang hymns glorifying God and fortifying themselves for the trials they were about to endure. From *The Martyrs Mirror* comes one such story where, in 1546, four Anabaptists were condemned to death and delivered to the executioner.

> When they were being led out to the slaughter, they boldly and joyfully sang. . . . The brethren then knelt down and fervently prayed, offering up this burnt offering as their final farewell to the world. . . . They then blessed each other, and exhorted one another to steadfastness, to be strong and of good cheer, saying, "Today we shall be together in the kingdom of the heavenly Father."[15]

With such a rich heritage, it should not be surprising that Mennonites today (and other people of faith as well) need to sing in order for our faith to be whole. What our interviews offer is a rough map or a kind of diagnostic grid for understanding the content and consequences of the spiritual encounters that occur in the midst of singing. One way of outlining that map is to say that as we sing, Mennonites are formed in faith in three fundamental ways:

- **Our vision of God is formed**—In singing, we encounter a revelation of the word of God—the living Word of the risen Christ as well as the written word of scripture.
- **We are formed into Christian community**—In singing, we discover ourselves bound in love to one another and to the body of Christ in many times and places.
- **Our life is formed as people of the spirit in the world**—In singing, we are transformed as we find comfort, healing, and new life that empower us to love and serve Christ in the world.

Such a grid or framework not only explains what happens when Mennonites sing but offers a guide for pastors, teachers, musicians, parents, spiritual mentors, and others who oversee the processes of spiritual formation. Interestingly enough, this same framework can also interpret the outcomes of other central actions of the worship. Preaching and praying, for example, can similarly form a vision of God, create Christian community, and empower worshipers to love and serve in the world. What our interviews demonstrate, however, is that among the various acts of worship, singing occupies a privileged place in the experience of Mennonite worshipers and thus requires special attention and care from those who lead the church and its worship.

Singing Forms a Vision of God

Encountering the Word

The starting place for spiritual formation is, of course, life in the Spirit. Without an encounter with God and a relationship with God, no new life emerges. According to the interviews, the encounter with God in song has two distinct dimensions: one is an encounter with the Word revealed in scripture or poetic texts; the other is direct, mystical experience of God's presence. In the first dimension, music plays a supportive and interpretive role as it imparts scripture and shapes a vision of God. In this dimension, hymns become a source of theology and the language of prayer.

When the Hymnal Council was at work creating the book that eventually became *Hymnal: A Worship Book*, George R. Brunk III, dean of Eastern Mennonite Seminary, gave a brief meditation one day at morning prayer. He referred to Samuel Johnson, the eighteenth-century dictionary maker, who said that if he were allowed to make the ballads of a nation, he cared little who made the laws. Further, Johnson noted that those who are permitted to make the hymns of the church need care little who preaches or makes the creeds. Hymn writers will more effectively mold the sentiments of a church than those who preach or make creeds or confessions. At the conclusion of his meditation, George shook his long finger at the members of the council and said, "Now be careful how you do your work today!"

How (and why) do hymns play such a powerful role in shaping our theology and our vision of God? Songs come to dwell in our imaginations in much the same way scripture does. The biblical sto-

O God, our help in ages past 328

ST. ANNE CM

1 O God, our help in a - ges past, our hope for years to come,
2 un - der the shad-ow of thy throne thy saints have dwelt se - cure.
3 Be - fore the hills in or-der stood, or earth re - ceived her frame,
4 A thou-sand a - ges in thy sight are like an eve-ning gone,
5 Time, like an ev - er - roll-ing stream soon bears us all a - way.
6 O God, our help in a - ges past, our hope for years to come,

1 our shel-ter from the storm - y blast, and our e - ter - nal home;
2 Suf - fi-cient is thine arm a - lone, and our de-fense is sure.
3 from ev - er - last - ing thou art God, to end-less years the same.
4 short as the watch that ends the night be - fore the ris - ing sun.
5 We fly for - got - ten, as a dream dies at the op'n-ing day.
6 be thou our guard while trou-bles last, and our e - ter - nal home.

Text: based on Psalm 90, Isaac Watts, *Psalms of David*, 1719, alt.
Music: attributed to William Croft, *Supplement to the New Version of the Psalms by Dr. Brady and Mr. Tate, 6th ed.*, 1708

ries we hear from childhood populate our heads with a cast of characters and create a holy geography in our minds. Ultimately these stories construct a vision of who God is, who we are, and what the relationship can be like—in other words, a theology. Sam Keen describes how the Bible stories of his childhood formed his history and theology:

> It was in Tennessee that I first learned about the history of my native land, in partition-divided Sunday school rooms covered with pictures and maps of the Holy Land. Before I was six I had walked through Judea, Galilee, Capernaum, Bethlehem, Jerusalem, sharing a dusty road with Jesus and the disciples, finding at day's end the comfort of a footbath, bread, and olives in a humble home.

And what a rich time and place it was to which I belonged! Over these hills and desert places my forebears—Abraham, Isaac, David, and Solomon—had roamed, killing the enemies of the Lord and establishing a kingdom for the children of promise. From papier-mâché models I learned the architecture of the Holy Land, and from bathrobe dramas its ways of dress (and at recess there was milk and graham crackers). I learned of Deborah's heroism (but not of Molly Pitcher's) and of the judges and kings the Lord raised to lead and chastise his people (but not of the judges of Blount County who helped to keep whiskey illegal and bootlegging profitable). I knew the topography of Judea before I could locate the Cumberland Plateau, as I knew the road from Damascus to Jerusalem before I could find my way from Maryville to Knoxville.[16]

If we start at the most literal level, we realize that we know and remember many of our sacred texts because of the memorable music to which they have been sung: for example, the beloved Psalm 23 can be found in a multitude of beautiful settings. Three examples from *Hymnal: A Worship Book* are an eighteenth-century Irish melody for "The King of love my shepherd is" (No. 170); a nineteenth-century Scottish tune, Crimond, for "The Lord's my shepherd" (No. 578); and Marty Haugen's late twentieth-century "Shepherd me, O God" (No. 519). Many other examples could be given of scripture texts—Jesus' words or poetry from the book of Isaiah, to name two—that appear in a variety of musical guises. In *Hymnal: A Worship Book*, for example, two contrasting musical settings give expression to the Beatitudes: "Oh, blessed are the poor in spirit" (No. 231) is a sonorous setting from the Russian Orthodox liturgy while "Blessed are the persecuted" (No. 230) uses a vigorous Tonga melody from Zambia.

What we sing comes to inhabit our imaginations and develops within us, first, a consciousness of God, then a relationship with God, and ultimately a response to the God we encounter as we sing. Not only do these texts become memorable because of mere repetition of words, they also live within us because of the music to which they are set.

Not only do the songs of the church imprint scripture on our minds, they also bring to life the narratives of scripture. It is significant that the largest section of *Hymnal: A Worship Book*, called "Proclaiming," comprises stories of scripture. People we interviewed fondly recalled hymns that told stories of the Good Shepherd searching for a lost sheep or of Jesus calming the storm at sea. We come to *love* the stories as we sing them, not just *know* them.

If we move beyond literal scripture texts, we find that hymns inhabit our imaginations in yet another way: poetry and evocative, image-filled texts also create a vision of God. One example is "Immortal, invisible, God only wise" (No. 70) and its climactic last sentence, which startles us with revelation:

All praise we would render,
  O help us to see
'tis only the splendor of light
  hideth thee.

Moving from transcendence to immanence, we find that the breadth and depth of God's care for all creatures is perhaps not better expressed anywhere than in the simple images of Swedish poet Caroline Berg's "Children of the heavenly Father" (No. 616):

Children of the heav'nly
  Father
safely in his bosom gather.
Nestling bird nor star in
  heaven
such a refuge e'er was given.

Marlene:
As a young adult, I once found myself unexpectedly in a hospital emergency room. Full of fear as I lay on a table in an examining room, I desperately tried to remember a scripture I could repeat to myself that would bring calm. Nothing came. Though I searched every corner of my mind, I couldn't remember a single text I had ever learned. After a few minutes, a hymn began singing itself inside me: "O God, our help in ages past, our hope for years to come, our shelter from the stormy blast, and our eternal home" (No. 328). I sang the song over and over again until peace returned. Later when I reflected on the incident, I felt chagrined that I had been unable to remember any scripture. I thought of how ashamed all my childhood Sunday school and Bible school teachers would be if they knew! Then I looked at the hymn text again and realized that it is a setting of Psalm 90. I had indeed remembered scripture—a text mediated through music. I also realized that in moments of panic one does not necessarily have access to information stored in the left brain; fear can stop those circuits from functioning. What I did have access to was something embedded more deeply still in my blood and bones—a song I had sung over and over again in worship.

Reflecting on the intimate relationship with God depicted in the text of "O thou, in whose presence" (No. 559)

> *Where dost thou, dear Shepherd, resort with thy sheep,*
> *to feed in the pastures of love?*

one person said gratefully, "I *have* that text because of the music."

An unusual image of God is found in the anonymous text of "The tree of life" (No. 509), in which each stanza ends with a phrase describing Christ as an "apple tree." While at first the image may simply seem quaint or colorful, it bears a much deeper meaning understood by the ancient and medieval church. In the thirteenth century, Bonaventure wrote:

> Picture in your mind a tree whose roots are watered by an ever-flowing foundation that becomes a great and living river with four channels to water the garden of the entire church. From the trunk of this tree, imagine that there are growing twelve branches that are adorned with leaves, flowers, and fruit. This is the fruit that took its origin from the Virgin's womb and reached its savory maturity on the tree of the cross under the midday heat of the Eternal Sun, that is, the love of Christ. In the garden of the heavenly paradise—God's table—this fruit is served to those who desire it.[17]

The church's wisdom and the poetic insights of individual poets, along with scripture's great treasury of images of God, provide abundant resources for nurturing faith's imagination. A song provides a spacious territory for exploration of this abundance, a space where "names for our God, dreams, signs, and wonders sent from the past"[18] can give us what we need to know and love God today.

Hymns not only speak *about* God, they invite us to speak *to* God. As demonstrated in previous chapters, hymns become the prayers of those who sing. Most people we interviewed resisted making a sharp distinction between singing and prayer; they were very clear that a Mennonite hymnal *is* a prayer book. Whether in personal prayer or corporate prayer, the songs we sing create an openness to God, they give us language for approaching God, they enable us to hear God, and they call forth our response to God.

Thus they contribute to the development of a relationship with God—an essential dimension of spiritual formation.

Meeting Mystery

> *Last night, after praying Compline in the darkness, the final verse of the last Psalm began to move around inside me, like the Spanish canto hondo—deep song. I found myself cooperating with this music, leaning into it, knowing that when its last note vanished into the silence, another leaf would be living on the tree I call "myself."*
> —Paul Marechal[19]

For many people, a second significant dimension of spiritual experience is direct apprehension of God's presence—what might be called mystical experience. In the course of ordinary living, such experiences occur in a variety of ways: some people encounter God in the beauty or terror of nature; others meet God in the presence of great art; some see divinity reflected in the face of a child or an aging grandparent; others find their inner selves awakened to the Spirit's presence as they wait before God in silence. Even though it was difficult for most of the Mennonites we talked with to find words for these experiences, it was clear that singing hymns is, commonly, one of the mystical approaches to God.

Marlene remembers the ordinary mysticism of Sunday mornings in her childhood:

In my memory, the hymn we often sang first was a nineteenth-century text and tune by Robert Lowry, "O worship the Lord" (No. 124). The first chord on the word O was always held for a dramatic moment before we moved on to sing the rest of the hymn. Women's voices, clear and soaring, sang a duet in the middle of each stanza; then the male voices joined them in the vigorous refrain, "Oh, glory hallelujah. . . ." When the song was finished and the last notes hung in the air, the presence of God was palpable—holiness was everywhere, mingling with the sunlight that danced above us.

Ken has a childhood memory of "To thy temple I repair" (No. 165, *Church Hymnal*):

To Thy Temple I Repair

165

I will come into Thy house in the multitude of Thy mercies.—Ps. 5: 7

JAMES MONTGOMERY, 1812   GUISBOROUGH 7. 7. 7. 7.   C. T. BOWEN

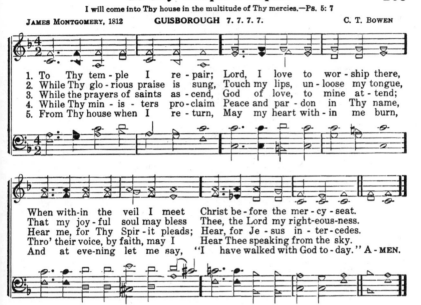

1. To Thy tem-ple I re-pair; Lord, I love to wor-ship there,
2. While Thy glo-rious praise is sung, Touch my lips, un-loose my tongue,
3. While the prayers of saints as-cend, God of love, to mine at-tend;
4. While Thy min-is-ters pro-claim Peace and par-don in Thy name,
5. From Thy house when I re-turn, May my heart with-in me burn,

When with-in the veil I meet Christ be-fore the mer-cy-seat.
That my joy-ful soul may bless Thee, the Lord my right-eous-ness.
Hear me, for Thy Spir-it pleads; Hear, for Je-sus in-ter-cedes.
Thro' their voice, by faith, may I Hear Thee speaking from the sky.
And at eve-ning let me say, "I have walked with God to-day." A-MEN.

To the child's mind and imagination, this hymn was peculiar. It had no melody (at least in the soprano), it had absolutely no rhythm, and it had interesting harmonies that were a real challenge to the singer. The text was filled with powerful images, some of which would surprise me when I heard them read from the Scripture.

In addition, this poem had a "here-and-elsewhere" quality: "temple" meant church, but likely not the one I was in; to have one's eyes touched and tongue unloosed was certainly more chaos than I had ever experienced. I liked the idea that even as the minister spoke, I might hear God really speaking from the sky. And while I never recalled my heart burning, I surely wanted it to! And could anyone possibly imagine a better way to end the day than to claim to have walked with God?

And if the here-and-elsewhere nature of the hymn were not enough by which to survive a long sermon (likely of little interest to this young soul), the quietness with which everyone sang this hymn was purely otherworldly. And there was the appended "Amen," one of the few amens we sang, even when they did appear in that hymnal. What a moment of unalloyed bliss to sing this little hymn.

At the heart of the matter, what singing does is to create openness to the moving of God's Spirit. In order to sing, one must breathe; in order to sing together, people must breathe together. Earlier in this chapter we noted Theophan's suggestion that if one wants to be filled with the Spirit, one should sing—and "singing will set alight the Spirit." Other writers have made similar assertions. Jewish writer Abraham Joshua Heschel said:

> Humanity is the cantor of the universe, and in whose life the secret of cosmic prayer is disclosed. To sing means to sense and to affirm that the spirit is real and that its glory is present. In singing we perceive what is otherwise beyond perceiving. Song, and particularly liturgical song, is not only an act of expression but also a way of bringing down the spirit from heaven to earth.[20]

Thomas Troeger, professor of preaching at Iliff School of Theology in Denver, writes,

> "Singing, not just listening to the music of others, but setting our own throat, mouth, ears, and head vibrating with the sound of God's praise is one of the most ancient and constant ways that the Spirit has been evoked."[21]

Why this connection between Spirit and song? How does singing set alight the Spirit?

Perhaps the book of Genesis provides a clue. In the very beginning when all was chaos, God sent a wind that swept and blew across the chaos. Wherever the Spirit of God breathed and blew, life came forth. And according to Job 38:7, what emerged was a song, "when the morning stars sang together and all the heavenly beings shouted for joy."

Before a child is born, the beat of a tiny heart is a sign of life; thus rhythm begins in the womb. After a child is born, its first act is to gulp for air, to breathe. The next act is a cry—to unloose a song. (At least that's what most parents think it is when their child is born!) The infant's next act is to search for food and drink. And so we are born—to breathe, to make a noise, and then to eat and drink.

The most powerful rituals are those that are most deeply embedded in human experience. They have a quality of inevitability about them because they spring from the most basic human actions. Perhaps the reason singing and the Eucharist have such a powerful hold on worshipers is that they are merely extensions of what we already know to be our deepest necessity.

In ancient Eucharistic theology, the holiest moment, the moment when heaven touches earth, is at the *epiclesis*, the prayer invoking the Holy Spirit to "come upon these gifts and make them holy, so they become for us the body and blood of our Lord, Jesus Christ."[22] The Spirit is invited to breathe again upon creation and bring life. Is it possible that this same enlivening is what happens as people sing?

Musician Joseph Gelineau uses a provocative image for singing in worship when he speaks of it as "God's daughter." He explains: "God gave music to mankind that it might signify the suffering and glory, the sacrifice and love of his Son who dies and lives among his brethren. It is a mystery of faith."[23] Thus, music is a sacrament signify-

So remember: just as the body of Jesus Christ was born by the Holy Spirit from the spotless Virgin Mary, so too the singing in the Church of God's praise, which is an echo of the harmony of heaven, has its roots in that same Holy Spirit. But the body is the garment of the soul and it is the soul which gives life to the voice. That's why the body must raise its voice in harmony with the soul for the praise of God. . . . God should be praised with crashing cymbals, with cymbals of clear praise and with all the other musical instruments that clever and industrious people have produced. For all the arts serving human desires and needs are derived from the breath that God sent into the human body. And that is why it is fitting that God be praised in all.

—*Hildegarde of Bingen*[24]

ing the love and grace of God expressed in the gift of his Son, and while the Eucharist reveals God's Son, the sacrament of singing reveals God's *daughter*. In both instances, it is the breath of the Spirit that animates the ritual action—in our breath and pulse as we sing, in our eating and drinking as we partake of the Eucharist.

Several people we interviewed seemed to have intuitions that went this direction. Describing what happens with chant singing, one said:

Chant allows you to enter a place of quietness that metered singing doesn't allow you to. It's a circular pattern that you let go around and around inside your body. That's how the Spirit enters. Singing doesn't put up any boundaries, doesn't get it down as clearly as words try to or even drawings do.[25]

Another person made a connection between breathing as prayer and what happens in singing:

In quiet prayer, one of the things you become aware of is your breath—just breathing and somehow breathing down into your body, which is what we do naturally when we are singing. We take breath in and then express it. It's cyclical, because it always comes back. . . . I probably feel the presence of God more clearly in music than in almost anything else in worship.[26]

Another person, struggling to find words for what happens when he sings, described his encounter with God in song:

[When we are] in the act of singing a song, God ministers to us. . . . God makes himself real to me and I think that is one reason he gave us music—[to use as] an avenue or tool to express our hearts to him and he in turn to express his presence to us. God's speaking to me is more real when it is coupled with music, more present.[27]

For a number of years we have led an annual weekend at Laurelville Mennonite Church Center in Mount Pleasant, Pennsylvania, with Mennonite music and worship leaders from across North America. It is billed as an exploration of music in worship. But one year, we heard that a number of people were referring to the event in terms of spiritual renewal. "You lure us here by promising that we'll learn how to lead music and worship better," one person told us. "Then we get here and discover we've come to a revival meeting!" We were not at all dismayed.

A similar story is told by Professor Don Saliers in *Worship Come to Its Senses*. He described a service for the renewal of baptisms in which "the singing was strong, the prayers fresh, and the preaching a powerful claiming of living out our baptismal life in Christ."

After the service one person responded, "Did we celebrate a sacrament here or hold a revival? I couldn't tell the difference!"[28]

Perhaps the point is that the two—sacrament and revival—are not fundamentally different. In both, the Spirit of God breathes and blows and brings new life. And in both, the transforming encounter creates a fresh vision for living in cooperation with God's purposes in the world.

Singing Forms Christian Community

> *Who hears music, feels his solitude peopled*
> *at once.*
> —Robert Browning[29]

In the midst of a treatise on the church, theologian Karl Barth asserts, "The community which does not sing is not the community."[30] Similarly, Leonard Sweet observes, "In the past, the church was a 'tuning' place where people could sing, chant, and intone together, thereby tuning their mindbodyspirits to their families, their village community, and their geographical place and time in history." He goes on to explain:

> A life silent of "joyful noises unto the Lord," or a worship life where others (whether choirs or soloists) make those noises for you, is a life lived out of tune; we become out of tune physically, mentally, morally, spiritually, and socially. Through the resonant fields created by liturgy, the whole person comes together and becomes alive through music, and from the heat of that aliveness individuals weld together to form a community. . . . It is by singing that we become a vibrating community, resonating with the divine music of the spheres.[31]

The physical act of singing together—the discipline of breathing and vibrating together—cannot be overestimated as an essential element of spiritual formation. Because Christianity claims an indissoluble link between love of God and love of neighbor (Mark 12:29-31), it becomes imperative for the Christian community to make that commitment audible and visible—first to ourselves and then to others. It may be that the recent popularity of monastic chant has to do not only with the mystical aura surrounding such music but with the fact that only a finely tuned community can produce such sounds—a gift missing from many people's lives as the twenty-first century begins.

Making sound together emphasizes interdependence and interconnectedness, what Anabaptists called *Gelassenheit,* the willingness to surrender one's self and strength to God and to others. When one person interviewed said "in losing yourself [in singing], you gain more for yourself," he touched on this very paradox. Another person described the delight and satisfaction that happens when people are willing to enter into singing: "When the Spirit has really been moving during a hymn, you can feel it at the end when people sit down, and you think, 'Ahhh.' "

People who make music together cannot be enemies, at least while the music lasts.
—Paul Hindemith[32]

Mennonites who were interviewed were acutely aware of diverse strands of connection that happen when they sing—connections with the universal church, with people of the past, their sisters and brothers in the faith, parents and other family members, someone they just happened to sit next to, the sensuality of men's and women's voices in harmony, and the many layers of emotional and spiritual connectedness in the congregation. This awareness of connection was illustrated by a group of students from Goshen (Indiana) College who were studying abroad for a semester in China. After being there a few weeks, they sent an urgent message home: "Please send us some Mennonite hymnals. In this strange land, we don't know who we are without our song books."

Those interviewed were also aware of the gifts of emotional and spiritual support they received through song. Most often remembered was the music sung at funerals or in the weeks and months following a death. Another time music seemed especially significant was at leavings and homecomings: As stated previously, one person reported not being able to sing in the weeks before she moved from her community; another compared the experience of returning home to Mennonite singing to sinking into a feather bed. Many,

many people exulted in the joy of ordinary singing week after week in Sunday morning worship—a precious and treasured gift.

Another important communal function of singing is the restoration of unity during or after conflict. People that we interviewed told stories of this happening both in informal settings and in large congregational meetings. A member of a worship committee at Seattle Mennonite Church gave this account:

> This year the worship committee has been composed of personalities that have not meshed as a working group. It's not been real outright so we could tackle it and address it, but it has been stressful. During the last couple of months . . . we've taken to singing at the beginning and close of each meeting. Something amazing has happened—singing has helped to lower some of the suspicions; it's like we're beginning to find common ground by singing together. That didn't happen when we began with devotions—scripture and talking and all that. It's been fun.[33]

In some congregations, singing is used as a mode of prayer in meetings of spiritual discernment. As a way of opening themselves to the Spirit's presence, one congregation chose to intersperse repetitions of the Taizé chant "O Lord, hear my prayer" (No. 348) with periods of silence while considering a decision they had to make.

Sometimes a hymn offers a community a way to express its sense of identity. "Praise God from whom" (No. 118) filled this role following its publication (as No. 606) in *The Mennonite Hymnal*. The cooperation required to sing this demanding hymn allowed Mennonites to dramatize their hope to be united before God as a harmonious, loving body.

In a world of vanishing international boundaries, the spiritual health of the body of Christ is nurtured when congregations sing music from a wide variety of ethnic and cultural groups. Thomas

We haven't yet managed a foretaste of the heavenly banquet to come: we cannot celebrate Christian unity by coming to the table together. But we can have a foretaste of the heavenly hymnfest to come. If we can sing together, eating together should not be too far behind.
—*Patrick Henry*[34]

Troeger says, "I believe part of our spiritual maturing as the church at the end of the twentieth century depends upon our singing the songs of Christians from other places and times."[35] Whether we can sing songs well is not nearly so important as the attempt to enter into another community's ways of expressing faith and their relationship with God, thus opening ourselves to new experiences of God and deeper unity in the church.

When we breathe together, we are bound together as one. In the yoking of ourselves in the common act of singing, our hearts are united in love and commitment to one another. Physically, spiritually, emotionally, singing indeed creates the body of Christ.

Singing Forms Our Life as People of the Spirit in the World

> *Quite in conformity with the ideologies of the entire Near East, music is not so much a thing of beauty as an ethical force.*
> —Eric Werner[36]

The spiritual formation of Christians is not complete if it involves only a relationship with God and other Christians. God intends the people of this new spiritual community to be salt and light in the world, a living sign or witness of the reign of God coming to be. If the church's ancient assertion is true—"first we sing, then we believe"—then one of the functions of singing in spiritual formation is to give us opportunities to speak our convictions, commitments, and hope, and to thus be empowered to live our faith with creativity and power in the world.

Singing hymns provides a time and place where we can express what our hearts truly desire in words and commitments we might not have the courage to speak apart from music. An example of this kind of hymn is "If all you want, Lord" (No. 512), by Carol Doran and Thomas Troeger. A reflection on the first commandment, the text is a mind game in which singers acknowledge all their reservations about loving God with heart, mind, strength, and soul. At the end of each of the first three stanzas, there is a short piano conclusion that brings the harmony back to a point of repose. In effect, it

O Gott Vater

AUS TIEFER NOT 87. 87. 887

33

O   Gott   Va - ter,
die   du,   O   Herr,

wir   lo - ben
so   gnä - dig   -

dich, und   dei   -   ne   Gü   -
lich, an   uns   neu   hast

te   prei   -   sen:
be   -   wie   -   sen,

und   hast   uns,

Herr,   zu   -   sam   -   men

g'führt, uns   zu

er   -   mah   -   nen   durch

dein   Wort, gib   uns

Ge - nad   zu   die   -   sem.

Text: Leenaerdt Clock, *Ausbund,* 17th c.
Music: based on the notations of J. W. Yoder in *Amische Lieder,* 1940 and Olen F. Yoder in *Ausbund Songs with Notes,* 1984.
         Adapted to current singing east of Goshen, IN, by Mary K. Oyer

communicates a completed act, even a sense of satisfaction. Then, in the last stanza, the poem says:

> But since, O God, you want them all
> to shape with your own hand,
> I pray for grace to heed your call
> to live your first command.

Upon arriving at the last stanza, singers find themselves realizing that, truth be told, they are far from singing the truth: they don't really love God with all their heart, mind, strength, and soul. But how they wish that they did! This time, the piano adds no conclusion. How it all will end is left hanging. More is required for the music's completion as well as for the fulfillment of the commandment. Here, metaphorically, is where grace is needed.

One person expressed similar ideas about another song, "In thee is gladness" (No. 114). "It's a sheer statement of faith, saying, 'You can strip me of whatever you want, but you can't strip me of my love for and knowledge of Jesus.' And that's there—no matter what," she said.

The songs we sing provide courage to live by our convictions even in dangerous or hostile times. A particularly poignant story comes from *Martyrs Mirror*. In Holland, in the summer of 1556, a tailor named Gerrit Hasepoot was sentenced to die for his faith. When his wife came to see him for the last time, she could hardly hold their infant in her arms because of her great grief.

> When he was led to death, and having been brought from the wagon upon the scaffold, he lifted up his voice and sang the hymn:
> Father in heaven, I call:
> Oh, strengthen now my faith
> Thereupon he fell upon his knees, and fervently prayed to God. Having been placed at the stake, he kicked his slippers from his feet, saying: "It were a pity to burn them for they can be of service still to some poor person." The rope with which he was to be strangled, becoming a little loose, having not been twisted well by the executioner, he again lifted up his voice and sang the end of the hymn:

Brethren, sisters, all, good-bye!
We now must separate,
Till we meet beyond the sky,
With Christ our only Head:
For this yourselves prepare,
And I'll await you there.[37]

In addition to their power to fortify in danger, hymns also have power to change and redirect a life. During Lent one year, Marlene visited Gethsemani Abbey, the Trappist monastery in Kentucky where Thomas Merton lived as a hermit. While hiking there, she came to a place called the Garden of Gethsemane. In the garden was a statue of Jesus kneeling in sorrow, and near it, a small memorial plaque:

Jonathan Myrick Daniels
1939–1965
Selma, Alabama

She couldn't remember the story of Jonathan Myrick Daniels, but she was curious about this young man whose death placed him in the company of Jesus in the garden.

The next winter while gathering materials for a worship service commemorating the life and death of Martin Luther King Jr., she came across Daniels' story. During the days of the Civil Rights movement, Daniels was an Episcopal seminarian in Cambridge, Massachusetts. One afternoon he went to a meeting of the student executive committee. While they sat around drinking coffee, they heard a report from a fellow student on his wife's plans to fly to Selma that night in answer to Dr. King's plea for northern volunteers. The committee voted to take up a collection to cover her expenses.

Daniels, a tall, lanky, dark-haired man with an actor's good looks, went back to his dormitory room to examine his conscience. Should he go to Selma? Could he spare the time? He finally concluded that the idea was impractical. He later wrote, "With a faintly tarnished feeling, I tucked in an envelope my contribution to the proposed Selma fund."

Later that evening Daniels went as usual to evening prayer. As he was singing the Magnificat,

> *God has showed strength with his arm,*
> *God has lifted up the lowly* . . .

he found himself "peculiarly alert, suddenly straining toward the decisive, luminous, Spirit-filled movement." He knew that he had to go to Selma. Quickly he packed his suitcase, rushed to Logan Airport where he found a seat on the same plane carrying other volunteers, and flew south.

Less than seven months later, Jonathan Myrick Daniels was dead, the victim of an Alabama segregationist's shotgun. A song had opened the way to a martyr's death.[38]

Patrick D. Miller Jr., Old Testament scholar at Princeton Theological Seminary, says:

> Any community that sings with conviction, "All people that on earth do dwell, sing to the Lord with cheerful voice; him serve with fear, his praise forth tell" cannot give its ultimate allegiance to a Hitler or a Kennedy or a Reagan or a political party of any stripe.[39]

Because we eventually become what we sing and pray, our loyalty will be reserved for God alone as the songs and hymns of the church shape us in that conviction and energize us to live our faith. Singing thus becomes the handmaiden of spiritual formation; it enables the church to receive and respond with joy to the love of Christ and to become a glorious sign of that love in the world.

Reframing the Conversation: Singing as Sacrament

The interviews demonstrated the power of singing to form faith in individuals and in the church. Pastors, parents, teachers, musicians—and all those who guide the spiritual formation of the next generations—often wonder whether music will have the same power to shape faith as traditional patterns of life give way to the rich but confusing pluralism of North American life.

In terms of this discussion, perhaps the most salient feature of postmodern life is its never-ending quest for direct personal experience. As trust in traditional authority erodes, people come to rely more and more on their own experiences of reality. A deep spiritual hunger emerges as people find themselves left alone and cut loose from the communal values of the past. In unexpected and sometimes bizarre ways, people seek a center.

One baby boomer who was interviewed said, "I think people love to cry. We have so few places where we can cry. It's so hard to be moved. In life you get so busy, and singing just brings you down to your heart, and it tells you exactly where you are."

At such a time, the church—if it is listening—has a unique opportunity to offer spiritual guidance. But this guidance must come in particular ways that respond to the hungers of the postmodern soul. The church cannot offer only an intellectual approach to faith, nor can it provide only affective experiences.

The postmodern soul longs for *integration*—of heart and mind, of transcendence and immanence. What neither Kathleen Norris nor Anne Lamott nor Sam Keen (nor many others) can tolerate is a worldview that splits reality apart. They want both clear thinking and warm feeling. They want both a cosmic God beyond the limits of their imaginations and a comforting, tender, healing presence that dwells within.

In the past, the sacraments of the church have been that place of convergence for heart and mind, body and soul. As water flows, oil is poured, or the bread and the cup are served, the Spirit moves within the entire person—and we know we have been met by the Holy One.

Two stories illustrate the singular power of sacraments to bring people into God's presence.

One person we interviewed told us of a woman in her thirties who had become dissatisfied with the sterile worship patterns of her Mennonite congregation. In her quest for something other, she began attending Sunday mass in a local Catholic parish, a religious tradition that was quite unfamiliar to her. When she asked the priest if she might participate in communion, he asked, "Do you believe in the presence of Christ in the world?" "Oh, yes, I do," she replied. "Then you are welcome at the table," he said.

The woman joined the Catholic community at prayer and gratefully received the bread and wine of the sacrament. After some weeks, she began to notice something peculiar. As she went about her work and daily routines, she became aware of a sensation of hunger. Even though she was well fed, by Friday of each week the feeling of hunger became intense.

During the Sunday morning liturgy, the sensation of hunger persisted and came to a climax when the congregation prayed, "Lord, I am not worthy to receive you; but only say the word, and I shall be healed." Then the woman would walk forward, receive the bread and wine, and find her hunger satisfied.

As an Anabaptist, the woman had no intellectual or theological constructs for explaining what happens in the Eucharist, yet Christ came to her in the simple act of eating and drinking. Her direct, personal experience (of which she was at first suspicious) provided all the opening that was needed for the healing mercy and grace of God to penetrate her life.

The second story was written by Kay Collette, who describes herself as possessing an education steeped in rationalism, and who found, in her mid-thirties, that her life was falling apart. As an agnostic and existentialist, she writes, she had no faith to provide a buffer or sense of meaning in the trauma of personal failure and family loss she endured. She says:

> On a rainy November morning, I went to the piano to practice a soprano aria from Handel's *Messiah* for an audition. After fifteen minutes of two-octave scales that were smooth as running water, I started singing, "Come unto Him, all ye that labor; Come unto Him, ye that are heavy laden, and He will give you rest." Carried by the ravishing melody, the words began to enter my very being like warm oil, bringing an invitation to rest. The habitual bodily anxiety began to melt away. A promise of rest seemed to float on the breath. The try-hard muscles of my upper back smoothed a little, softening the hero shoulders, easing the long-term, low-grade tension in the gut. It was as though a love I had never known was pouring forth from within me. Only months later did I recognize this moment as the beginning of my conversion. It was a bodily experience of incarnation, a gut knowledge of the surpassing love of Christ.

> Six months later I walked into an unfamiliar church known to

have an altar call. Responding to the invitation to "Come unto Him," I went forward. Had that invitation come through a sermon or the written word, it would have been killed off by the dragons who guarded the door of my rational worldview. But something about a song is nearly irresistible in that it reaches both the mind and the heart, the former with meaning, the latter with beauty. It has taken me a long time to realize that of the two, the heart is the larger source of intelligence for me.

Eventually, Collette found her way to a seminary to study. There, her faith in a living Christ was deeply challenged by historical-critical studies: Was there indeed a resurrection? Is Christ God? An intense struggle became unbearable at a Christmas Eve Eucharist and haunted her until New Year's Eve when she went to bed "with a despair darker than any in memory."

Before dawn on the first day of the new year, the despair returned. But in the middle of the dark, I noticed a melody. A song was playing inside my head. After having breakfast and cleaning the kitchen, the song was still there. I recognized the title—it was "Love divine, all loves excelling," not Hyfrydol (No. 178, among others), but Beecher (No. 592), the tune we sang back in Tennessee. I took the hymnal to my prayer place in the back room and sat down to read the words:

> *Love divine, all loves excelling,*
> *joy of heav'n to earth come down,*
> *fix in us thy humble dwelling,*
> *all thy faithful mercies crown!*
> *Jesus, thou art all compassion,*
> *pure unbounded love thou art;*
> *Visit us with thy salvation,*
> *enter ev'ry trembling heart.*

Like lectio lasers, certain phrases cut through the bars of skepticism—"Breathe thy loving Spirit into every troubled breast, let us all in thee inherit, let us find thy promised rest." Those words in that long-forgotten melody addressed the greater intelligence of my heart with a knowledge deeper than logic; the hymn gave me the words my heart longed to pray—Jesus, you who are pure unbounded lover, enter this trembling heart. This time it was I who invited him to "Come." The rational dragons surrendered their totalitarian hold to the astonishing power of a majestic old hymn. I knew with my muscles and bones that the hymn was a prayer formed in me by the Holy Spirit. It was a final surrender into mystery for the sake of a lover I could not live without.[40]

Two stories of God's love being poured out in needy human hearts—one through a traditional sacrament of the church, the other through the sacrament of singing. In both stories, it was the postmodern inclination to trust the power of a personal experience that opened a doorway to the sacred and brought freedom and release.

Yet the obvious limitation of personal experience is its subjectivity. Because every human life is unique, personal experience is limited by the particulars of any given history. But even with these limitations, the desire of postmoderns for personal experience clearly represents an open door through which the church can introduce people to the reality of God.

If the responses of Mennonites in our interviews are valid, then the experience of hymn singing in worship can and does satisfy the deep need for a personal encounter with the sacred in a way that engages the whole person: body, heart, and mind. Not everyone will be comfortable using the term "sacrament" for what happens when we sing: The traditional aversion to the term among Mennonites may make it unusable for some. But without the traditional language of sacramental theology, it has been difficult for Mennonites to validate the very real spiritual significance of this important act of worship. With our strong preference for ethics and a gritty determination to live our faith in ordinary, daily ways, the church has been malnourished or underdeveloped when it comes to mystical communion or beauty that calls forth adoration and praise—or at least, underdeveloped in its discussion of such things. Thus it may be that Mennonite detachment from the sacramental tradition has caused us to overlook what is the most obvious and powerful locus of God's presence in Mennonite worship: hymn singing.

By whatever name we call it, if we choose to recognize its power and then make sufficient place for Spirit-inspired singing in Mennonite spiritual formation, we will provide a sturdy foundation for the faith of the next generation. Mennonites have sung their prayers of confession and praise; have sung their longing for healing and transformation; have sung joy; and, around fresh graves in the church cemetery, have sung their hope in the resurrection. Without our music, the faith of many—the interviews suggest—would be barren. Instead, music gives us a faith with flesh and blood and breath and ushers us into realms of glory and grace.

If we keep on singing, we will know (with Sam Keen) that the Lord is still our Shepherd because our songs will set the truth quivering in our bodies, minds, and souls. Singing will bring us into the presence of the Shepherd who leads into green pastures and beside still waters to the eternal feast of God's presence.

We, your children in your likeness,
share inventive pow'rs with you.
Great Creator, still creating,
show us what we yet may do.

—*Catherine C. Arnott*[1]

Part Four

What the Song Is Becoming

What is this place

1

KOMT NU MET ZANG 98. 98. 966

1 What is this place where we are meet-ing? On-ly a house, the
2 Words from a-far, stars that are fall-ing, sparks that are sown in
3 And we ac-cept bread at his ta-ble, bro-ken and shared, a

earth its floor, walls and a roof shel-ter-ing peo-ple, win-dows for
us like seed. Names for our God, dreams, signs, and won-ders sent from the
liv-ing sign. Here in this world, dy-ing and liv-ing, we are each

light, an o-pen door. Yet it be-comes a bod-y that lives when
past are what we need. We in this place re-mem-ber and speak a-
oth-er's bread and wine. This is the place where we can re-ceive what

we are gath-ered here, and know our God is near.
gain what we have heard: God's free re-deem-ing word.
we need to in-crease: God's jus-tice and God's peace.

Text: Huub Oosterhuis, *Zomaar een dak boven wat hoofden*, 1968; tr. David Smith, ca. 1970
Music: *Nederlandtsche Gedenckclanck*, 1962; harmonized by B. Huijbers, 1968

The Story of a Song

Songs are thoughts, sung out with the breath when people are moved by great forces and ordinary speech no longer suffices. Man is moved just like the ice floe sailing here and there in the current. His thoughts are driven by a flowing force when he feels joy, when he feels fear, when he feels sorrow. Thoughts can wash over him like a flood, making his breath come in gasps and his heart throb. Something like an abatement in the weather will keep him thawed up. And then it will happen that we, who always think we are small, will feel still smaller. And we will fear to use words. But it will happen that the words we need will come of themselves. When the words we want to use shoot up of themselves—we get a new song.

—Orpingalik, a Netsilik Eskimo[2]

Much of the music of *Hymnal: A Worship Book* has found its way into the singing repertoire of congregations very quickly. A prime example is the first hymn in the book, "What is this place." Its entrance into the Hymnal Council's work, into the book, and into a new canon of important hymns is a rich and varied story.

"What is this place" was introduced to North American churches at the annual meeting of the Hymn Society in the United States and Canada at Bethlehem, Pennsylvania, in July 1986. Robert J. Batastini, general editor and project director for *Worship III*, was introducing that book just before its publication. Richard Proulx, organist for the event, played a very cheerful pseudo-Renaissance dance prelude on the tune, complete with sprightly recorder and nasal krummhorn sounds. His delightful and imaginative playing caused people in that congregation to turn around to watch. We all smiled, and we all sang with great delight and enthusiasm. (Proulx's prelude is included in the *Accompaniment Handbook* to *Hymnal: A Worship Book*.)

Several on the Hymnal Council were at that event. Ken's memory

Ken:

In January of 1993, my mother died after a lengthy battle with cancer. Though she was never physically able to attend worship services between the time the hymnal came out and the time of her death, she did familiarize herself with the contents of the new book. Shortly before Christmas of 1992, when I saw her for the last time, we were talking about funeral plans again. She wanted lots of singing at her funeral and very little talk. I asked once more what she would like to have sung. "It doesn't really matter," she said. "Just sing! But I do have one request." And, after reciting from memory all three stanzas of "What is this place," she said, "What a wonderful hymn! I especially like the phrase, 'We are each other's bread and wine.' That's the only hymn I would like to request that you sing."

It was the first hymn we sang at her funeral. Every time I sing that hymn, I sing with and for my mother, I remember and hear her words, and I remember her tears and can recall the heat of my own. But even when the words swim across the page because of those memories, I know the words: I gave her the book, but she taught me the words.

of it is of an intensely physical response, a knowing that grabbed from deep within him, a hearing of this hymn as an expression of something significant about his people. Others on the committee had similar responses, and within a very short time the hymn was considered by the entire Hymnal Council. It was subsequently accepted.

As we lived with this hymn throughout the hymnal-making years, its significance seemed to increase. However, conventional wisdom had it that the first hymn in a new hymnal shouldn't be new to congregations. "What is this place" was new to all three traditions involved in the hymnal, but it held an important theological concept for all parties and had already been introduced and enthusiastically sung after it appeared in the *Hymnal Sampler*, a preliminary selection of prospects for the book. Rebecca Slough, managing editor, made "What is this place" her choice for the new No. 1, and, when the committee first saw the hymns in an assigned order, they agreed. Conventional wisdom was wrong in this case; it was a right decision then, and it continues to seem right.

Many Mennonite congregations soon sang the hymn as though it were their own. In some places, people sang all three stanzas from memory just a short time after the book appeared. We seemed to recognize, in a hymn by someone from outside our tradition, something that met and matched our own inner conviction about the church. The music did not seem strange; simplicity of tune and of harmony were not foreign to our tradition of singing in four parts. Mennonites sang it as if we had rediscovered an article of value that had been lost or misplaced. In fact, at least one person had to be told that the song had not been in previous Mennonite hymnals. Before long, people told us that "What is this place" had found an important place in their lives. Rebecca Stoltzfus Miller described the phrase "we are each other's bread and wine" as "an image to sustain a generation." Adam Shenk, the youngest of our interviewees, cited "What is this place" as a favorite that he had "enjoyed singing all my life."

The Hymns We Borrow

"What is this place" is borrowed from the Roman Catholic tradition. It has long been a tradition for Mennonites to borrow hymns from others, and these borrowings often become the characteristic sounds of an era of our hymn singing. The hymnal with which a generation grows up is the book to which members of that generation most often refer when asked about their favorite hymns. Some interviewees could cite the page numbers of favorites from *The Mennonite Hymnal* (1969), *Church Hymnal* (1927), *Life Songs No. 2* (1938), *Church and Sunday School Hymnal* (1902), or even *Songs of the Church* (1953), *Our Hymns of Praise* (1958), or *Sing and Rejoice* (1979). There is no question that the hymns in each of these books significantly affected the sound of hymn singing for a generation.

The Mennonite Hymnal introduced a number of new sounds into Mennonite congregational singing. Hymns from early American sources were prominent in that book and were often mentioned as favorites: "O thou, in whose presence" (No. 273, *Mennonite Hymnal*/No. 559, *Hymnal: A Worship Book*), "What wondrous love is this" (No. 163 *MH*/No. 530 *HWB*), "Oh, how happy are they" (No. 272 *MH*/No. 597 *HWB*), "My Shepherd will supply my need" (No. 63 *MH*/No. 589 *HWB*), and "Hark! the glad sound!" (No. 112 *MH*/No. 184 *HWB*). These hymns were not entirely new to

Mennonite singers, having come from the singing school book traditions, especially *Harmonia Sacra.*

The choral hymn section of *The Mennonite Hymnal* included a number of hymns that offered special challenges to congregations: "Praise God from whom" (No. 606 *MH*/No. 118 *HWB*), "Jesus, priceless treasure" (No. 600 *MH*/No. 595 *HWB*), "All hail the pow'r of Jesus' name" (No. 601 *MH*/No. 285 *HWB*), "Break forth, O beauteous heav'nly light" (No. 609 *MH*/No. 203 *HWB*), William Billings' Easter Anthem ("The Lord is risen indeed," No. 613 *MH*), and "This joyful Eastertide" (No. 614 *MH*/No. 276 *HWB*). New also for Mennonite singers were the rhythmic versions of Reformation-era chorale and psalm tunes like "Lord Jesus Christ, be present now" (No. 91 *MH*/No. 22 *HWB*) and "Comfort, comfort, ye my people" (No. 121 *MH*/No. 176 *HWB*), as well as a few hymns from non-Western cultures. Congregations enthusiastically took up the challenges and still count these hymns among their favorites.

And there were newer strains. Two hymns by Mennonite composers offered twentieth-century sounds to the ears and voices of congregations in the decades after 1969: Randall Zercher's "I bind my heart this tide" (No. 353 *MH*/No. 411 *HWB*) and J. Harold Moyer's "I sought the Lord" (No. 228 *MH*/No. 506 *HWB*). They also offered singers significant musical challenges; again the challenges were met, and these hymns remain among the most frequently listed favorite hymns.

This openness to and acceptance of new songs that Mennonites learned from *The Mennonite Hymnal* helped prepare the way for some of the singing done from *Hymnal: A Worship Book.* "Open, Lord, my inward ear" (No. 140, a Charles Wesley text to Bradley Lehman music) was listed as a favorite by a number of people. "Wind who makes all winds" (No. 31, a Thomas Troeger text to Carol Doran music) appeared several times in people's lists of favorites. Both of these were mentioned by people young and old.

"Mothering God, you gave me birth" (No. 482, a Jean Janzen text to Janet Peachey music) received an astonishing number of mentions in these interviews. For some, the text was a most welcome and long overdue set of images that people found helpful—even necessary—in completing their understandings of the nature of God. There were those, women especially, for whom this hymn offered healing for various wounds. In some places, the hymn has been used as a part of the recovery of wholeness following the painful separations of divorce. One woman found comfort in the phrase "hold me in faith until I flower." She described her own faith journey as a sometimes hopeless, sometimes plugging-away kind of trek, and welcomed the idea that God would indeed hold her as she and her faith flower. In often surprising settings, "Mothering God" has been selected as a favorite hymn when congregations have been given opportunity to choose.

Other hymns new to *Hymnal: A Worship Book* have succeeded because of rich harmonies similar to those found in traditional Mennonite singing. For example, the few hymns from the Russian Orthodox tradition are already widely sung. These songs are notable not only for their four-part sonorities, but for the reflective, meditative way they can be used in worship. "Who is so great a God" (No. 62) was suggested for hymnal consideration by a number of North American Mennonites to whom this majestic liturgical piece was introduced on a trip to the former Soviet Union. "Kyrie eleison" (No. 144), also a rich and harmonic piece, has found widespread favor in surprising ways. Mennonite antipathy toward liturgical language is long standing. Mennonite detachment, which in this simple refrain is impossible, is also well known. So when this little (on the page) but big (in experience) "Kyrie" was used at the 1991 General Assembly of the Mennonite Church in Eugene, Oregon, it was at least mildly astonishing to hear Mennonites singing it passionately, many with tears streaming down their faces.

"Kyrie eleison" no doubt appeals to Mennonites on many levels. First, of course, is the sound—the layers of rich harmony. It is also satisfying to sing an ancient text, the same prayer used by Christians from the earliest days of the church and based on the cry of blind Bartimaeus, "Jesus, Son of David, have mercy on me." Throughout the world even today when Christians find themselves in need of mercy and grace, they pray, "Kyrie eleison." Perhaps what happens in such a prayer is that we encounter the collective unconscious described by Jung. We connect with the deepest prayer of all human beings—the prayer that pleads for God's mercy and grace.

Hymns representative of the international church were few in number in *The Mennonite Hymnal*, but the ones that were there were valued. *Hymnal: A Worship Book* includes many hymns from the world church, more than most other recently published hymnals. Mennonites' experiences at Mennonite World Conference have been enriched by the important inclusion of song, instrumental music, and dance from many parts of the globe. Many of the attendees at the 1990 Mennonite World Conference in Winnipeg passed wish lists of international hymns to members of the hymnal committee. These hymns speak clearly to the many Mennonites who have spent time in cultures around the world in a wide variety of mission and service work.

Songs are sneaky things. They can slip across borders. Proliferate in prisons. Penetrate hard shells. . . . I always believed that the right song at the right moment could change history.

—*Pete Seeger*[3]

Of the many arguments that can be made for including this music in the hymn repertoires of North American Mennonites, none speaks louder than this one fact: Out of the total worldwide Mennonite and Brethren in Christ population, 45 percent are of European descent and 55 percent are from the rest of the world. Furthermore, the Kenyan Conference of Mennonites is second in size only to the Lancaster Conference of Mennonites. And, if more evidence were needed, within the Lancaster Conference alone, worship occurs in thirteen languages on any given Sunday morning.

Many of the hymns of the international church have found their way into the affection of singers. The African hymns are appealing for their introduction of rhythm as a "new" (for Mennonites!) musical element. Hymns of Native Americans have been widely accepted, sung, and enjoyed for their sense of awe and wonder, an astonishing thing considering that they are single-line, unaccompanied melodies that lack harmony—a "sacred" musical element for most Mennonites. One young man who was baptized on Easter

Sunday in 1997 asked his congregation to sing "Father God, you are holy" (No. 78). He said that his experience of finding God's love during his high school years was most accurately reflected in this hymn.

Hymns from Spanish cultures and Asian cultures are finding places in the worship of North American congregations. Hymns from African-American sources (spirituals and gospel) have awakened interest in vocal improvisation within a tradition that has prided itself on its music reading skills and on its interest in "doing it right." Young people have less difficulty with improvisation, as it is an important element in popular music. This music also presents us with another musical sound of community, one in which one's individuality is validated by finding a place in the varied sound of the group, or in Melva Costen's words, "We are, therefore I am."[4]

One of the nearest yet most distant cross-cultural experiences that awaits Mennonites in this hymnal is "O Gott Vater" (No. 33). Always the second hymn sung in any Amish service, it carries important memories for Mennonites who were formerly Amish. From the early seventeenth-century Anabaptist hymnal, the *Ausbund*, this hymn bears its singers back, deeply into memory, to a place modern singers rarely have the opportunity to venture.

There are more unison melodies (like "O Gott Vater") in *Hymnal: A Worship Book* than Mennonites have traditionally sung. *The Mennonite Hymnal* had introduced one type of unison hymn—a single line accompanied by keyboard. Two of these hymns from the British tradition have become favorites of many: "For all the saints" (No. 395 *MH*/No. 636 *HWB*) and "God is working his purpose out" (No. 605 *MH*/No. 638 *HWB*). At the time, this raised questions about what singing in unison would do to Mennonite four-part singing. Some found the new hymns difficult to accept; they wanted four parts.

In the decades between *The Mennonite Hymnal* and *Hymnal: A Worship Book*, many new hymns in this style appeared. Sometimes composers stated a specific intention for their unison hymns: that the unity the church has to offer could be signified by singing in unison—literally, as one voice—within this, our increasingly divided society.

These newer unison hymns come not only from British organ-accompanied sources ("Lift high the cross" [No. 321]), but also from popular song sources ("Here in this place" [No. 6], "You are salt for the earth" [No. 226], "New earth, heavens new" [No. 299]) and from other twentieth-century American sources ("Through our fragmentary prayers" [No. 347] and "The kingdom of God" [No. 224]).

One unison hymn that has been used in many settings is Natalie Sleeth's "In the bulb there is a flower" (No. 614), originally written to offer children an understanding of the mysteries of death. Used for funerals, weddings, and other varied occasions, it is a remarkable example of a hymn that speaks to difficult and intangible questions of doubt and faith in a comprehensive manner. One interviewee asked that the epitaph for her own life be drawn from this text.

Also new to *Hymnal: A Worship Book* are the fourteen titles from Taizé, plus the Taizé-like "Oyenos, mi Dios" (No. 358). Of all the music for worship that was created in the twentieth century, none captures the imagination of so wide a range of worshipers as does the music of Taizé. From those who would be utterly charismatic to those who would be utterly Episcopalian, this music has been received and embraced with enthusiasm.[5]

Like some other new songs, Taizé hymns take a simpler approach to the language used for singing: fewer words, more repetition, and easier entrance into "praying" the hymns than when many and complicated stanzas of text are available. One interviewee referred to his Pentecostal background as a tradition where a chorus was sung over and over until one was no longer thinking about the chorus or the words. He said:

> One could go deeper in prayer, saying something like, "God, you really know that it's hard for me to say these things but you know my heart, and there's all this stuff in there, and I don't want to mention it, but it's there, and I'm worried about it."

In the repetitions, he said, he found the place where he could both touch and release some of those difficult things. He said:

I can hardly think about "O Lord, hear my prayer" (No. 348) without getting tears in my eyes. You sing it for a while, and then you start to get beyond it and really open yourself up. With this music of Taizé, one ceases being a singer after several repetitions and becomes a singing listener. When the singing continues, I don't have to worry about making the music happen. For me it's a release to be opening up to God: "Here, take me, you know who I am." Then the cleansing process begins. Clock time ceases to exist; there can be no concern for moving on with the "agenda" of worship at those times.[6]

Ken remembers that when he grew up, it was common for churches to have two hymnals in the racks: *Church Hymnal* (which seemed to bear the imprimatur of "official" hymnal) and *Life Songs No. 2* (which seemed to be the one to sing from when singing with greatest pleasure). When *The Mennonite Hymnal* appeared, it took the place of *Church Hymnal*, yet *Life Songs No. 2* remained in the racks in many places. And when *Hymnal: A Worship Book* replaced *The Mennonite Hymnal*, there were still churches that kept *Life Songs No. 2* alongside it in the racks. The 1992 book included a number of hymns from *Life Songs No. 2*: "O worship the Lord" (No. 124), "Wonderful grace of Jesus" (No. 150), and "Great God of wonders" (No. 149), for example. Reaching back to include remembered hymns from before the 1969 *Mennonite Hymnal* reflected the power of those hymns to persist in the memory, even though they were not found in the current hymnal. It also reflects a cyclic view of history, one that resembles the Slinky toy, in which all things are indeed connected, and in which when a spot on this metaphor of history and time is touched, it affects the rest of the coil as well. The ways in which people embraced hymns such as these and "In thy holy place we bow" (No. 2) from the *Church Hymnal,* as well as "In the rifted Rock I'm resting" (No. 526) from the *Church and Sunday School Hymnal,* support an understanding of hymn singing experiences as formative and sturdy and serve to remind us of the size and span of time of the community of which we are only an immediate part.

Hymnal: A Worship Book contains seeds for significantly affecting the sound of Mennonite singing in the future. Like other hymnals of the decade, the breadth of music to be found in the book asks singers to hear and to produce sounds in worship besides those to which they have become accustomed. Attentiveness to the new will have its effects on the way things are done, and the situations that result will not always be comfortable. But the "new" in hymn singing will find its place among the old, and comparisons between it and the past will prove useful to our understanding of what happens when we sing. Sometimes we will value the familiar, sometimes replace it, and, in some cases, find place for the new among that which is already honored.

There remains no reason, except the laziness of leaders to lead and of worshipers to lift their eyes and ears, that hymn singing should ever be a dull event, given the millennium of Christian expression in text and music and the multiplicity of cultural responses to the gospel found in the new generation of hymnals. Ours is a diverse and varied humanity; Christ's is also a diverse and varied body.

True to Tradition and Open to the Future

In the few years since the appearance of *Hymnal: A Worship Book*, there is evidence that one of the real gifts this book has offered to the denomination is, in the words of one book publisher, "in having gotten us to sing from the same book again." Like other modern American denominations, Mennonites have been torn apart over issues centering around music. Strong opinions from every direction have been explicit about what shall and what shall not be sung. Perhaps it is a fair observation that this hymnal has offered the possibility of a "both/and" rather than an "either/or" approach to music. The "both/and" approach tends to be more inclusive in terms of the types of music in the hymnal and more communal in that we are encouraged to sing each other's songs. The "either/or" approach tends to keep us caught in a permanently unsettled argument—one that keeps us from singing until something is finally decided.

There are those who would describe (and market) this "both/and" approach as "blended" worship. The obstacle here is that someone has invented yet one more simplified product to sell to congregations earnestly searching for help with their worship. The problem (and challenge) is that "both/and" will require congregations to find out for themselves what their worship patterns, their style of language, and their canon of music will be. Unless changes in worship patterns are organic and true to the congregation's identity, they will never be accepted or valid. Many congregations are making these changes already; however, not many of us are comfortable yet because there are few reliable models to follow. Nor are there hierarchical voices of approval that will come from outside the congregation to tell us what to do.

What congregations face is the challenge the church of Jesus Christ has always faced: how to be true to the faith handed down to us and also true to the context in which we live out that faith. In the case of worship, both the old songs and worship patterns from the past as well as the many new songs and creative worship possibilities of the present are needed to fully express the rich, many-dimensioned, and multicultural nature of the church as we move into a new millennium.

According to Princeton professor Patrick D. Miller, one of the reasons we gather to worship is "to remind ourselves in prayer and praise that the secular ability to live in a world without taking account of God is neither the last word nor the right one. The praise of God is the last word of faith. . . . In praise, God gives us the last word."[8] In response to all God offers us—in creation and in the incarnation—we offer our songs of praise, and we indeed have the last word.

"**T**hrough song," said the Rebbe, "you climb to the highest palace. From that palace you can influence the universe and its prisons. Song is Jacob's ladder forgotten on earth by the angels. Sing and you shall defeat death; sing and you shall disarm the foe."
—*Elie Wiesel*[7]

Even the powers of evil cannot destroy that last word—the people's song of hope and praise.

In 1973, in Santiago, Chile, the democratically elected government of Salvador Allende was overthrown by General Pinochet, whose military junta became known for brutal human rights abuses. During the takeover, 25,000 citizens were herded into the capital's sports stadium and held under arrest at gunpoint while, hour after hour, people were singled out to be taken below to be beaten. It was a scene of naked evil triumphant.

But one of the people in the arena was Victor Jara, a Chilean folk singer who was one of the most popular in all of South America. He had his guitar with him, and so into the midst of the destruction of democracy and the terror of violence, a song was heard. The crowd hushed as they heard a familiar voice. Their fears subsided as they listened to songs of courage and hope. Though they were defeated, they began to believe again.

The soldiers could not let this go on. They went up to Mr. Jara and said, "If you don't stop that song, we'll cut off your hands." Victor looked them in the eye and kept strumming his guitar. He could not keep from singing. So they cut off his hands. Then they laughed at him saying, "Now try to play your guitar." He could not, but Victor Jara could still sing. And so, a cappella, he sang. The song went on. He couldn't keep from singing. The song went on and on until finally the soldiers fired their machine guns at him to make it stop.

They killed the man, but they could not kill the song. As long as the junta ruled, the people would continue to sing of Victor Jara.[9]

As long as God gives breath, and beyond, we will keep on singing.

166   I'll praise my Maker

NASHVILLE 888. 888

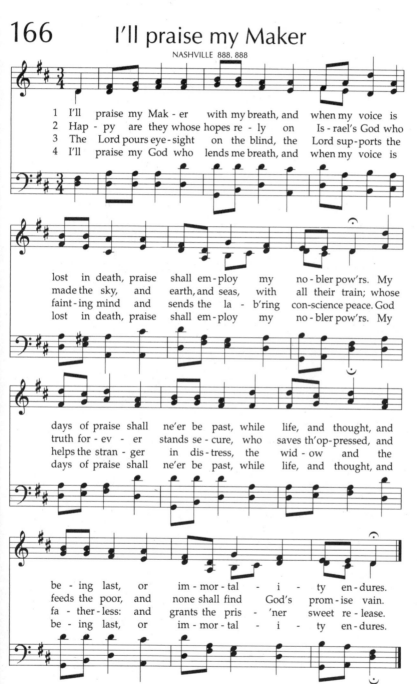

1 I'll praise my Mak - er with my breath, and when my voice is
2 Hap - py are they whose hopes re - ly on Is - rael's God who
3 The Lord pours eye-sight on the blind, the Lord sup-ports the
4 I'll praise my God who lends me breath, and when my voice is

lost in death, praise shall em - ploy my no - bler pow'rs. My
made the sky, and earth, and seas, with all their train; whose
faint - ing mind and sends the la - b'ring con-science peace. God
lost in death, praise shall em - ploy my no - bler pow'rs. My

days of praise shall ne'er be past, while life, and thought, and
truth for - ev - er stands se - cure, who saves th'op-pressed, and
helps the stran - ger in dis-tress, the wid - ow and the
days of praise shall ne'er be past, while life, and thought, and

be - ing last, or im - mor - tal - i - ty en - dures.
feeds the poor, and none shall find God's prom - ise vain.
fa - ther - less: and grants the pris - 'ner sweet re - lease.
be - ing last, or im - mor - tal - i - ty en - dures.

Text: Isaac Watts, *Psalms of David*, 1719, alt.
Music: Lowell Mason, *The Choir, or Union Collection of Church Music*, 1832

[The book of Revelation]
asks us to believe that only
the good remains, at the end,
and directs us toward
carefully tending it here
and now. We will sing a new
song. Singing and praise will
be all that remains. As a poet,
that's a vision, and a promise,
I can live with.

—*Kathleen Norris*[1]

Epilogue

What Have We Learned?

What have we learned from these interviews and from our experiences of singing with congregations during the course of this project? A general answer to this question would call attention to the complex act of singing and the interconnected levels of activity that song generates. It is necessary to have a song; it is better if that song carries with it the memory of a significant time and place where it was sung with others; it is even better if one's song is sung here and now with anyone who will join in. More specifically, we can say that Mennonite song is a precious gift, and one that requires care.

1. Care for What Is Sung

First, **care for what is sung** and how it is sung is not misplaced care. More explicitly, those responsible for the leading of hymn singing in their congregations cannot take their responsibilities lightly or fail to meet the demands of their positions. Time after time, we have heard people affirm that singing is of utmost importance as a communal act of worship, that singing would be the last element of worship to be surrendered, that both the act and all the resonances of singing are critical to the spiritual formation of individuals and communities. People sing together and in so doing are engaged by the act of singing itself; this should be a challenge to song leaders—not a free pass. Further evidence beyond the people's word here is not needed.

2. Care for Images and Metaphors

Second, because those who sing hymns attach so many levels of meaning to them and because so many events are dated by the hymns that were sung on a particular occasion, care must be taken for the **images and metaphors** that are available to people. The book of Psalms, the model throughout history of what a hymnal should be, includes the gamut of human emotion and experience. Limiting ourselves in our singing to only praise or adoration or happy endings does not square with real life. When trouble strikes, when there is cause for anger, should war or strife or pestilence or flood assail, hymns should be available that allow the expression of human responses to these events. Expressions of praise and trust in God are certainly appropriate at such times. But if the psalmist is to be trusted, there is also value in expressing in the presence of God and of the community all those angers, doubts, hurts, and fears. A hymnal or a congregation's repertoire of hymns that does not include the entire range of human emotions is not complete.

3. Care for the Craft of Music

Third, there must be **care for the craft of the music** that is offered to people for singing. Special demands are made of music that is to be sung by a congregation instead of a soloist. The demonstrated need for people to sing things over and over before they become ingrained in their innermost souls asks that music for the congregation be worthy of many repetitions. At the conclusion of her interview, Shirley Yoder Brubaker observed:

> Perhaps the only trouble with new hymns is that they have no associations by which the people claim them. Time and repetition are required of the music that will eventually move to the center of people's experience.[2]

Unfortunately, the church music scene, like the popular music scene, is currently an industry whose livelihood depends on today's tunes becoming tomorrow's castoffs. No era in church music has been without its transient, more popular music. But no era except ours seems to be influenced by the idea that either one uses old and out-dated traditional song or uses new and contemporary song. That is not a choice we need to make; there is space for both, and what deserves to stay around for the next generations will stay, and what deserves to wither by the wayside will blow away like dried grass. This evolutionary process happens on its own and is not subject to the wishes, tastes, or needs of any of us.[3]

4. Care for the Church's Role as Patron of the Arts

Fourth, it may seem impossible to imagine that the church might ever recover at least part of its **role as a primary patron of the arts.** It is no secret that the relationships between church and art have been rocky. The common understanding is that the arts (and artists) left the church, although a convincing argument can be made that it was the other way around: The church left the arts. The arts, especially music, have a direct attachment to the worship practices of all religions of the world, and for Christians to have drawn such sharp lines of separation between themselves and the arts robs the Christian tradition of a portion of its birthright.

When Western culture in the middle of the eighteenth century chose to draw sharp distinctions between the sacred and the secular and to elevate the secular over the sacred, too much in the church's history was given away. Johann Sebastian Bach was perhaps the last great Western musician for whom all was sacred and available for the service of God. But now when the masterworks of Bach and others are taught in educational settings, they are often separated from their roots in the church, its history, its liturgy, its people, and its song.

On the surface, this may seem a plea on behalf of cultural matters, but it is really an important theological matter. How we view the arts in the context of our life of worship speaks of our belief in our Creator's power to make and to inspire, in our Creator's power to endue us with like power, and the right of our Creator to have our creative efforts returned in praise to the One who gave them.

Should Bill Moyers be the one who makes a very fine video about the power of "Amazing grace," or should it have been the church? Should Sweet Honey in the Rock be the group that insists on the connections between the gospel and social and political justice, or should it be the church? Should concert halls around the world be responsible for the preservation of the crown jewels of church music, or should it be the church? And for all that is yet to be imagined and created and discovered, should it not be the work of the church to be involved in the imagining, the creating, and the discovering rather than waiting around to imitate what the outside world produces?

5. Care for Hospitality Toward Another's Song

Fifth, the musical world in which we live expands along with the rest of the world around us. Communications being what they are, it is increasingly less possible to avoid each other's songs. Ultimately it is an act of hospitality to **learn one another's songs.** We find communal space when, in unexpected ways and places, "they know my song" or "I know their song." Technology exists that enables each of us in our own small worlds to create our own hymnals, containing only the songs we want to sing. Such technology should be resisted. There are times when for reasons of solidarity it is important to be able to sing each other's songs. There are times when we need to sing these songs on behalf of those who cannot sing for themselves.

We often hear of intense conflicts over what shall be sung. One of the most surprising revelations in these interviews was the overwhelming number of people who said there was nothing they couldn't sing in worship, that while there may be some things not much to their liking, they could nevertheless sing with sisters and brothers for whom those songs were important.

6. Care for Time Spent Singing Together

Sixth, we need to **care for how much time we spend singing together.** It is characteristic of our culture that we seem to prefer watching others do things rather than engaging in these activities ourselves. Furthermore, we can pay others (often very well) to perform for us. Time after time in these interviews, the people told us of the importance of using the breath, of singing with a community, of the space that singing created for the soul. One person who had spent several years as a part of Quaker congregation said that he learned to love the silence deeply, but he hated "the not singing."

Most of us in our churches sing much less than we used to. Not only do we meet less frequently, but we also sing less when we are together. Other aspects of worship have found space in worship, often at the expense of congregational singing. Our interviews do not support reducing the amount of time given over to singing together. If singing is as important as we claim it is in our tradition, we will need to find ways of making more time for singing, of teaching our children to sing, and of strengthening the abilities of many of us to sing more confidently. Mary Oyer once observed:

> We have a wonderful heritage. I think we will keep it only if we sing. We have to sing much more. We have to practice by doing it. Sing more. Keep singing. Sing. Sing. Sing. Sing before church. Sing during church. Sing after church. Just do it![4]

The singing of the congregation is the most important music that happens in worship. It is a potentially subversive truth (though often selectively ignored) that nearly everything that needs to be done in corporate worship can be done (and has been done) by singing together. The professional world of church music, however, seems to overlook this point. Brochures for major church music conferences across the country include offerings for all kinds of musical life in the church, but rarely anything having to do with congregational singing.

Singing, as we have heard from these interviews, is a complex matter, even when the singer is not aware of the complexities. None of us can function fully and equally efficiently at all the levels of potential involvement with a hymn; few of us can function on more than one level at a time. Therefore, we return to sing a hymn again and again, and in doing so, certain elements that we thought familiar can be renewed to our surprise, delight, and edification. The pleasures of singing are enormous, and the rewards of turning that pleasure toward the praise of the Creator who gave us that gift are infinite.

7. Care for the Voice
as an Instrument

For an increasing number of people, the human voice must be recovered as the primary musical instrument and as a prime means of spiritual expression. There are many reasons for this, including the tendencies of society toward spectatorship, but also, more importantly for the church, the wrong messages that have been delivered to the singers in the congregation. Those of us who lead music are often guilty of telling singers that their voices are not needed. Those who lead music with their hands or with their voice and those who accompany with instruments—acoustic or electric—bear the enormous **responsibility for caring for the voices** of those who sing in the congregation.

Matters of courtesy are often overlooked—how singers are invited into the singing, how they are allowed to breathe at ends of phrases and between stanzas, how they are taught what they need to know for singing. Accompaniments should give to the singers the character, the tempo, and the style for the singing of the hymns; they should not mislead. Electronically amplified sounds of voices or instruments often privilege those who have the amplification over those who do not. These sounds ensure that the music will continue, regardless of whether the people in the congregation sing.

When it becomes clear to a congregation that its voices are not needed, it will most likely choose not to sing. The acoustics of the room and the space they provide or fail to provide the voice to be heard in the community are also a major consideration. It ought to be clear that if singing matters, the singer matters also.

8. Care for the Tradition

Finally, it should be very clear from the interviews that **singing in the Mennonite tradition** is a very important matter. Myron Augsburger observed in his travels around the world that

> when you meet with Mennonite workers, you usually meet around a hymnal. This was a common sense of community and fellowship. Singing together, bonding with other people is very, very impor-

tant. When we went to Washington to plant a church, we had no congregation. I bought a couple dozen *Mennonite Hymnals* so that in starting this fellowship, we could fuse a common ground of music along with the Bible and other dimensions of worship.[5]

In a guest editorial for *Mennonot*, a journal for younger Mennonites not sure how Mennonite they are, Marshall King told this story:

> On Labor Day weekend 1995, twenty to thirty [Eastern Mennonite University] grads gathered near Harpers Ferry, West Virginia, to be together. It started as a way to say good-bye to three of us who were headed overseas for three years with Mennonite Central Committee. So for three days, we ate and played and laughed and remembered how we're human and need each other.
>
> On Sunday morning, we sat in a large circle and pulled out the blue hymnals. For almost two hours, we sang and shared and laughed and cried. That room held people at different places in their faith journey and a healthy share of Mennonots. But for two hours, we were one, a community of friends singing the songs of our youth and our future.
>
> We sang 606 by heart, the same way our children will.[6]

Again and again in the interviews we were reminded to treat this tradition with respect and not to discard it lightly. Sue Williamson became a Mennonite as an adult, having been raised in the Disciples Church. At the end of a conversation with her and a number of other Seattle Mennonite Church folk, she said:

> I sometimes get the sense from people who have been raised in the Mennonite tradition that they don't fully understand and appreciate what singing brings to their faith in ways not present in other denominations. I am always amazed, during these last four years spent worshiping in the Mennonite church, to go to other denominations and find that this singing and what it offers is just not as present in their worship services. It is something which is delegated to the professional musicians and the choir. It's a wonderful gift, and I wonder if Mennonites realize that.[7]

The gift has brought us much, perhaps even sustained our faith at times it might otherwise have fallen apart. Take the songs. Give yourself to the singing of them, but take the songs into your heart, into your life, into your community, and into your soul. "I do not have any brilliant conclusions to end this story other than a few simple observations," John Paul Lederach said at the conclusion of his story about "God of grace and God of glory":

> When you choose to walk in the path of justice, peace and recon-
> ciliation, take heart in knowing the path has been walked by
> others before you. Make sure to hold the hand of good friends
> who will walk at your side. Take a song with you. Put it deep
> inside so that no matter what happens, its seed can burst forth
> when you most need it. And know that it is the God of grace
> and the God of glory who breathes life into the seed and light
> onto your path.[8]

Notes

Origins of the Singing Project

1. This sentence comes from Cornelius Eady, "Paradiso," in *You Don't Miss Your Water* (New York: Henry Holt and Co., 1991), 32–33. In context, it is as follows:

In Italy, a scholar is giving an after-dinner talk on her study of Dante and the many questions left unanswered about the afterlife.

For example, where does the shade of the body, the one true and indestructible rainbow vessel, go to wait for the end of time if the head goes one way at the moment of death, and the limbs another?

And I thought of my father, fired to dust in a plain urn, and all the answers I'd learned in church, how all the lost must rise, commuters home at last, from wherever fate has ditched them, with their dishonored ropes and blown equipment, up from the sea, the peat, the misjudged step, the angry fuselage, the air bright from ashes, as will and memory knit.

Will my father's glorified body be the one I'd grown up with, a stocky man, perhaps dressed in his one good suit?

Will he be the young boy I'll never know, Sonny Eady, who wanders off for months at a time, always returning with no account of his movements?

Will he be the groom my mother saw, or the shape of the man she claims visited her weeks after his funeral, appearing just to help my mother close this file on their lives, just to tell her *fare-thee-well, woman, I'll never see you no more?*

How can this be done? is one question the scholar is here to work on, and as she places our hands into Dante's, and night gathers in the mountains, I think that every hymn is a flare of longing, that the key to any heaven is language.

2. Albert Barnes, *Barnes' Notes on the New Testament*, ed. Ingram Cobbin (Grand Rapids, Mich.: Kregel Publications, 1962), 1075.

3. *Hymnal: A Worship Book* (Elgin, Ill.; Newton, Kan.; and Scottdale, Pa.: Brethren Press, Faith & Life Press, and Mennonite Publishing House, 1992). Both Ken and Marlene served on the Hymnal Council that produced *Hymnal: A Worship Book*. In addition, Ken served as the music editor for the hymnal, and Marlene was a member of the project's Worship Committee. Hymn numbers given throughout this book are from *Hymnal: A Worship Book* unless otherwise noted.

4. Throughout the book, the names of those interviewed generally are given for longer quotations. The speakers of shorter quotations have usually not been identified because these selections tend to represent "the voice of the people" in a more general sense. In some cases, names were withheld to protect the speaker's privacy.

5. May 1997, The Graduate Theological Foundation, Donaldson, Ind.

Part One

1. Ann Graber Hershberger, interview, 31 October 1994.

2. *The Mennonite Hymnal* (Newton, Kan., and Scottdale, Pa.: Faith & Life Press and Mennonite Publishing House, 1969).

3. Mary Oyer, *Exploring the Mennonite Hymnal: Essays* (Newton, Kan., and Scottdale, Pa.: Faith & Life Press and Mennonite Publishing House, 1980), 23–24.

4. George R. Brunk II, interview, 31 October 1994.

5. Linda J. Clark, *Music in Churches: Nourishing Your Congregation's Musical Life* (Alban Institute, 1994), 71.
6. Isaiah 6:1.
7. Brian Friel, *Dancing at Lughnasa* (New York: Dramatists Play Service Inc., 1993), 83–84.
8. Henry Buckwalter, interview, 29 November 1994.
9. Daniel Suter, interview, 2 September 1994.
10. "PAX boys" were conscientious objectors who volunteered to go to Europe to rebuild towns and villages in the aftermath of World War II.
11. Lee Snyder, interview, 11 November 1994.
12. Chuck Neufeld, interview, 11 October 1994.
13. Michael Bay, interview, 29 November 1994.
14. Esther Augsburger, interview, 8 September 1994.
15. Ron Guengerich, interview, 3 November 1994.

Part Two

1. Gustave Flaubert, *Madame Bovary*, trans. F. Steegmuller. Part 2, Chapter 12, 208.
2. Cynthia Lapp, written interview, 14 January 1995.
3. The poem Jean refers to is Herbert's "The Pearl."
4. Jean Janzen, interview, 21 October 1994.
5. Lee Snyder, op. cit.
6. Marilyn Houser Hamm, interview, 23 October 1994.
7. Merle Good, interview, 28 November 1994.
8. In the video *Lift Every Voice & Sing* (Harrisonburg, Va.: Brothers & Sisters Production, 1995).
9. Shari Miller Wagner, "A capella," *Menno Expressions* (6 February 2000), 2. This poem was first published in *Southern Poetry Review*.
10. Janzen, op. cit.
11. Shirley Yoder Brubaker, interview, 8 September 1994. *Life Songs No. 2* was edited by S. F. Coffman and published in 1938 by Mennonite Publishing House (Scottdale, Pa.).
12. Lois Kauffman, "My favorite hymn—and why," *Timbrel* (May/June 1998), 12.
13. Stanley E. Kropf, Marlene's husband, wrote this poem in 1993 in preparation for a fiftieth birthday party for him and six of his cousins, who all turned fifty the same year and had grown up together in Harrisburg, Oregon.
14. This line is from the refrain to "Come, we that love the Lord" (No. 14).
15. The "little red children's songbook" is *Our Hymns of Praise*, J. Mark Stauffer, ed., (Scottdale, Pa.: Herald Press, 1958).
16. Hamm, op. cit.
17. Justina Neufeld, interview, 15 October 1998. More of Justina's story is told in "A Family Remembers," *Mennonite Life* (March 1990).
18. Ron Guengerich, op. cit.
19. Eleanor Kreider, interview, 30 December 1994.
20. Joetta Handrich Schlabach, 30 January 1995.
21. Ted Swartz, interview, 12 January 1995.
22. This poem was written by Luella Wolfer Nice, Marlene's mother, and quoted in a letter from Luella's cousin, Mildred Schrock, on 25 November 1994.
23. "Shaped notes" are just that—notes with heads printed in various shapes depending on their rank in the scale. In the United States from the eighteenth century on, shaped-note systems (most used either four or seven shapes) were a popular way of teaching beginners to read music. For example, a square-headed note—called *la*—would, in a four-shape system, be used for the third and sixth elements of the scale. The most popular shaped-note hymnals (used to this day) include *The Harmonia Sacra* (first printed in 1832) and *The Sacred Harp* (first printed in 1844). More recently, some editions of *The Mennonite Hymnal* were printed in shaped notes.
24. Guengerich, op. cit.

25. Good, op. cit.
26. Hamm, op. cit.
27. Brunk, op. cit.
28. Joanne Sprunger, interview, 4 October 1994.
29. Kreider, op. cit.
30. Eric Bishop, interview, 28 November 1994. Michael Bishop is Eric's brother.
31. Chuck Neufeld, op. cit.
32. Mary Lehman Yoder, interview, 20 October 1994.
33. Wanda Teague, interview, 16 November 1994.
34. Jody Moyer, interview, 28 November 1994.
35. The Grateful Dead's Jerry Garcia, quoted in *A Sourcebook About Music*, Alan J. Hommerding and Diana Kodner, compilers (Chicago: Liturgy Training Publications, 1997), p. 40.
36. Laurence Martin, interview, 11 November 1994.
37. Snyder, op. cit.
38. Shirley Yoder Brubaker, op. cit.
39. Shirley Showalter, interview, 25 August 1994.
40. This is the refrain to "Lord, I am fondly, earnestly" (No. 514):
    Open the wells of grace and salvation
    pour the rich streams deep into my heart.
    Cleanse and refine my thought and affection,
    seal me and make me pure as thou art.
41. Phyllis Pellman Good, interview, 28 November 1994.
42. Zem Martin, interview, 29 November 1994.
43. Janzen, op. cit.
44. Ellis Croyle, interview, 16 October 1994.
45. Barbra Graber, interview, 2 September 1994. Barbra refers to stanza 3 of the hymn:
    Could we with ink the ocean fill,
    and were the skies of parchment made;
    were ev'ry stalk on earth a quill,
    and every man a scribe by trade;
    to write the love of God above
    would drain the ocean dry;
    nor could the scroll contain the whole,
    though stretched from sky to sky.
46. Graber, ibid.
47. Mary Lehman Yoder, op. cit.
48. Shirley Sprunger King, interview, 9 May 1995.
49. Mary Lehman Yoder, op. cit.
50. Jeffrey Shenk, personal conversation, 30 October 1997.
51. Taizé songs, many of which appear in *Hymnal: A Worship Book*, come from an ecumenical community centered in France, southeast of Paris. There are additional Taizé communities in a number of cities around the world. Many of the communities serve as retreat centers, and the different backgrounds of the people that come make it all the more important to create a sense of a body at worship. The songs of the community help make this possible. The music is melodically and harmonically simple and typically involves repetitive refrains, ostinatos, and canons, sometimes beneath a melody sung by a soloist or small group. Instrumental parts exist for most of the songs, but these are optional; the harmony can support itself without additional decoration. The effect is meditative; in the repetition of the choruses, worshipers find time to encounter the ideas and the feelings that the sound raises in their minds and souls. There is no limit to the repetitions and, at the same time, no limit to the musical and spiritual variations a group may find in them.
52. Janzen, op. cit.
53. Michael Bishop, interview, 28 November 1994.
54. Kreider, op. cit.

55. Graber, op. cit.
56. Croyle, op. cit.
57. Ruth Johnston, written interview, 9 May 1995.
58. Reta Halteman Finger, written interview, 28 January 1995.
59. Jacob W. Elias, written interview, 9 May 1995.
60. Jerry Derstine, interview, 2 December 1994.
61. Jean Weaver, personal correspondence, January 1995.
62. Snyder, op. cit.
63. Elaine Jantzen, interview, 5 November 1994.
64. This is an excerpt from a chapel address, "God of grace and God of glory," given by John Paul Lederach at Eastern Mennonite University on 13 March 1998.
65. Janzen, op. cit.
66. Janet Berg, interview, 15 October 1994.
67. Twila K. Yoder, "My favorite hymn—and why," *Timbrel* (May/June 1998), 12.
68. George Brunk III, "When my life is almost gone," *Crossroads* (Spring 1996), 30.
69. Kreider, op. cit.
70. Jeanne Murray Walker, interview, 15 August 1995.
71. Copy of address provided by the speaker.
72. Nell Kopp, written interview, 26 January 1995.
73. Mary Lehman Yoder, op. cit.

Part Three

1. Anne Lamott, *Traveling Mercies: Some Thoughts on Faith* (New York: Pantheon Books, 1999), 65. Copyright © 1999 by Anne Lamott. Used by permission of Pantheon Books, a division of Random House, Inc.
2. Karen Armstrong, *A History of God: The 4,000-Year Quest of Judaism, Christianity, and Islam* (New York: Alfred A. Knopf, 1993), xix.
3. Eugene H. Peterson, "Spirit Quest," *Christianity Today* (8 November 1993), 28.
4. Henri Nouwen quoted in Arthur Boers, "What Henri Nouwen Found at Daybreak," *Christianity Today* (3 October 1994), 29.
5. Kathleen Norris, *The Cloister Walk* (New York: Riverhead Books, 1996), 218.
6. Lamott, op. cit., 46–48.
7. Sam Keen, *Hymns to an Unknown God: Awakening the Spirit in Everyday Life* (New York: Bantam Books, 1994), 5–6.
8. Roger Hutton, "Is Singing Believing?" in *BBB Music Magazine* (April 1995), 51–52.
9. Leonard Sweet, *Faithquakes* (Nashville: Abingdon Press, 1994), 63–64.
10. Colossians 3:16.
11. Augustine divided sacraments into sacraments of the word and sacraments of action: sacraments of the word included sermons, prayers, and the reading of scripture; sacraments of action included water and wine, blessings, and rituals. All helped make divine realities present to anyone who understood the meaning of the signs. See further discussion in Joseph Martos, *Doors to the Sacred: A Historical Introduction to Sacraments in the Catholic Church* (New York: Doubleday & Company, 1982), 55–60.
12. Quoted in Gabe Huck, ed., *A Sourcebook About Liturgy* (Chicago: Liturgy Training Publications, 1994), 35.
13. From *The Art of Prayer: An Orthodox Anthology*, quoted in *A Sourcebook About Liturgy*, ibid., 36.
14. Quoted in *A Sourcebook About Liturgy*, ibid., 33.
15. Thielman J. Van Braght, *Martyrs Mirror* (Scottdale, Pa.: Herald Press, 1950), 475.
16. Sam Keen, *To a Dancing God* (New York: Harper & Row, 1970), 8–9.
17. Quoted in Gabe Huck, Gail Ramshaw, and Gordon Lathrop, eds., *An Easter Sourcebook* (Chicago: Liturgy Training Publications, 1988), 106.
18. This is a line from "What is this place" (No. 1).
19. Paul Marechal, *Dancing Madly Backwards* (New York: Crossroad, 1982), 7.

20. Quoted in *Prayers of Those Who Make Music*, David Philippart, comp. (Chicago: Liturgy Training Publications, 1995), 17.

21. Thomas H. Troeger, "The Hidden Stream That Feeds: Hymns as a Resource for the Preacher's Imagination," *The Hymn* 43, No. 3 (July 1992), 12.

22. The epiclesis, a prayer invoking the Holy Spirit's presence at the Lord's Supper, normally contains three elements: 1) an appeal for the Holy Spirit 2) to transform or sanctify the bread and wine 3) so that they may benefit those who partake of them worthily. The particular form of the prayer quoted here is from *The Roman Missal* and is based on *The Apostolic Tradition of Hippolytus*, 215 C.E. For further discussion, see John H. McKenna, "The Epiclesis Revisited," in *Eucharistic Prayers: An Ecumenical Study of Their Development and Structure*, ed. Frank C. Senn (Mahwah, N.J.: Paulist Press, 1987).

23. Joseph Gelineau, *Voices & Instruments in Christian Worship*, trans. Clifford Howell (Collegeville, Minnesota: The Liturgical Press, 1964), 27.

24. Quoted in *Hildegarde of Bingen's Book of Divine Works With Letters and Songs*, ed. Matthew Fox (Santa Fe: Bear & Co., 1987), 358–359.

25. Graber, op. cit.

26. Karen Moshier Shenk, interview, 7 November 1994.

27. Shawn Erb, interview, 26 November 1994.

28. Don E. Saliers, *Worship Come to Its Senses* (Nashville: Abingdon Press, 1996), 16.

29. Quoted in *A Sourcebook About Music*, op. cit., 10.

30. Karl Barth, *Church Dogmatics*, IV, Part Three, Second Half, trans. G. W. Bromiley (Edinburgh: T. & T. Clark, 1961), 867.

31. Sweet, op. cit., 64–65.

32. Quoted in *A Sourcebook About Music*, op. cit., 119.

33. Mary Beth Stueben, interview, 15 October 1994.

34. Patrick Henry, "Singing the faith together," *Christian Century* (21–28 May 1997), 501.

35. From a speech at Music and Worship Leaders Weekend, Laurelville Mennonite Church Center, Mount Pleasant, Pennsylvania, 13–15 January 1995.

36. From *The Sacred Bridge*, quoted in *A Sourcebook About Music*, op. cit., 118.

37. Van Braught, op. cit., 560.

38. Quotations and story from Jack Mendelsohn, *The Martyrs: Sixteen Who Gave Their Lives for Racial Justice* (New York: Harper & Row, 1966), 196.

39. Patrick D. Miller, Jr., "In Praise and Thanksgiving," *Theology Today* XLV: No. 2 (July 1988), 188. The hymn quoted is No. 42.

40. Kay Collette, "Spirit's Songs," *Presence: An International Journal of Spiritual Direction* I: No. 2 (May 1995), 65–66.

Part Four

1. Lines from "God, who stretched the spangled heavens" (No. 414).

2. "Songs are Thoughts," quoted in Robert Bly, James Hillman, and Michael Meade, eds., *The Rag and Bone Shop of the Heart: A Poetry Anthology* (Harper Perennial, 1993), 162.

3. Quoted in *A Music Lover's Diary*, Shelagh Wallace and Scott McKowen, comps. (Willowdale, Ontario: Firefly Books Ltd., 1966), 130.

4. Adapted from several Melva Costen workshops and books, including *African American Christian Worship* (Nashville: Abingdon Press, 1993). On page 22 of that book, she writes "A cardinal point in the understanding of this African view of community is the adage: 'I am, because we are; and since we are, therefore I am.'" The quote she cites is taken from John S. Mbiti, *African Religions and Philosophy* (New York: Anchor/Doubleday, 1970), 141.

5. See note 51 to Part Two for more information on the Taizé community and its music.

6. Bay, op. cit.

7. Quoted in *Prayers of Those Who Make Music*, David Phillippart, comp. (Chicago: Liturgy Training Publications, 1995), 49.

8. Patrick D. Miller, Jr., "In Praise and Thanksgiving," *Theology Today* XLV: No. 2 (July 1988), 188.

9. Hope Douglas J. Harle-Mould, "How Can I Keep From Singing?" *Church Worship* (July 1992), 13–14.

Epilogue

1. Norris, op. cit., 220.

2. Shirley Yoder Brubaker, op. cit.

3. Thomas Troeger and Carol Doran speak helpfully on these matters in their discussion of ephemeral, conjunctural, and structural elements of music and worship in "Maps and Images" in *Trouble at the Table: Gathering the Tribes for Worship* (Nashville: Abingdon Press, 1992).

4. In the video *Lift Every Voice & Sing*, op. cit.

5. Myron Augsburger, interview, 8 September 1994.

6. Marshall King, "Defenses and dreams of a Generation Xer," *Mennonot* No. 9 (Spring 1997), 5.

7. Sue Williamson, interview, 4 October 1994.

8. From a chapel address at Eastern Mennonite University, 13 March 1998. The rest of the story appears in Part Two.

Hymn Index

Hymn title	Page number	Hymn number**
A wonderful Savior is Jesus	40, 73	598
All hail the power of Jesus' name	51, 142	285
All the way my Savior leads me	90	MH 573
Amazing grace!	159	143
Away in a manger	39	194
Be thou my vision	40	545
Blessed are the persecuted	113	230
Break forth, O beauteous heav'nly	142	203
Cast thy burden upon the Lord	92	586
Children of the heavenly Father	75, 114	616
Christ who left his home in glory	82	283
Come, O Creator Spirit, come	102*	27
Come, O thou Traveler unknown	93	503
Come, thou Almighty King	23, 82	41
Come, thou long-expected Jesus	131	178
Comfort, comfort O my people	142	176
Day is dying in the west	84	MH 493
Father eternal, Ruler of creation	93	MH 447
Father God, you are holy (Ehane he'ama)	145	78
For all the saints	145	636
For God so loved us (Gott ist die Liebe)	32*, 33, 57, 77	167
Go to dark Gethsemane	82	240
God is here among us	93	16
God is working his purpose out	145	638
God moves in a mysterious way	74	MH 80
God of grace and God of glory	86*, 87–90, 164	366
Great God of wonders	147	149
Great is thy faithfulness	29, 30–31*	327
Hark! The glad sound!	141	184
Have thine own way	51–52	504

* Denotes page where the hymn is reproduced
** Unless otherwise noted, all numbers refer to *Hymnal: A Worship Book*, 1992.
MH = *Mennonite Hymnal*, 1969
CH = *Church Hymnal*, 1927
LS = *Life Songs No. 2*, 1938

The Authors

Marlene Kropf is associate professor of spiritual formation and worship and director of spiritual formation at the Associated Mennonite Biblical Seminary in Elkhart, Indiana. She is also minister of worship and spirituality at Mennonite Board of Congregational Ministries. She served as a Mennonite Church representative on the Hymnal Council that produced *Hymnal: A Worship Book*.

Kenneth Nafziger is professor of music at Eastern Mennonite University in Harrisonburg, Virginia. He is artistic director and conductor of the Shenandoah Valley Bach Festival in Harrisonburg; the Lake Chelan (Washington) Bach Feste; Voce, a chamber choir in Reston, Virginia; Winchester (Virginia) Musica Viva, also a chamber choir; and the Charlottesville-Albemarle (Virginia) Youth Orchestra. He was music editor for *Hymnal: A Worship Book* and editor of the *Accompaniment Handbook*.